Watercolors

From Dürer to Balthus

Watercolors

From Dürer to Balthus

by
Jean Leymarie

BOOKKING
international

First published 1984
First paperback edition 1990

© 1995 by Editions d'Art Albert Skira S.A., Geneva

Reproduction rights reserved by A.D.A.G.P. and
S.P.A.D.E.M., Paris and PRO LITTERIS, Zurich

Printed in Switzerland by
IRL Imprimeries Réunies Lausanne s.a.

Library of Congress Cataloging in Publication Data

Leymarie, Jean
    Watercolors: from Dürer to Balthus.

    Translation of L'Aquarelle.
    Includes index.
1. Watercolor painting - History. I. Title.
ND1760.L4913 1984   759   84-50809
ISBN 2-605-00298-5

Contents

Paul Cézanne
(1839-1906)

Rocks at Château Noir, c. 1900.
Watercolour and pencil.

Introduction

Watercolour painting, done with pigments bound with a medium soluble in water, is the oldest technique of all, and was the most widely used before the appearance of oil painting. It differs from distemper or size painting; from tempera, which is painting with an egg-yolk emulsion; and of course from pastels, a contrary process of painting in dry colours. Its surface is paper, its instrument the brush, and the colour pigments are thinned in water and bound with gum arabic, a binding vehicle obtained from a species of acacia. By watercolour is meant transparent colours applied to the white or light-toned paper, parts of which may be left in reserve. In this it differs from gouache or body-colour, which is thicker and opaque, the colours being bound with glue, with an admixture of white pigment for lighter tones. Watercolours are applied from brighter to darker, gouache in the contrary way, the darker underpainting being gradually lightened. The two media may seem mutually exclusive, but in fact they are often used together, the watercolour being heightened with gouache.

The illuminations on the vellum pages of medieval manuscripts and the portrait miniatures painted on vellum at the Renaissance, and later on ivory, are technically akin to watercolour and gouache, but stylistically they are distinct from them. Natural pigments soluble in water were known in prehistoric times, but the decisive invention of paper was made by the Chinese, at some time in the early Christian era. It was also the Chinese who invented, or at least perfected, the soft-haired brushes used for writing, drawing and painting. Far Eastern painting, chiefly landscapes in washes of ink or light colours, is like the quintessence of watercolour by virtue of its limpidity, light-toned grounds and atmospheric respiration around a central void of positive value. But colour, with the Chinese, is deliberately reduced in scope and remains subordinate to line, to the aerial palpitation of signs (though there did exist an "ink splash" technique), while the Western watercolour, whether monochrome or bright, aspires to a spontaneity of colour handling, governed by no prior design. Pictorial in essence, and not linear, it is based on the radiance of light and the fluidity of bright colours in their infinite range of variations and suggestiveness.

This book, whose value lies first of all in the choice and quality of its illustrations, offers a survey of watercolour painting and its somewhat discontinuous history, with its privileged moments, its successive centres and its main fields of application. The diffusion of paper in Europe during the fifteenth century, after its long slow advance from the East, was a precondition for the wider practice of drawing and the rise of watercolour. For the latter, paper is not only the surface, but enters into its very substance and radiance. Its grainy whiteness absorbs and transmutes the flow of colours. The success of a watercolour depends on the right kind of paper and the right mixture of pigments and water.

Some sheets heightened with watercolour have come down to us from those model books that began to be used from the end of the International Gothic movement. But the independent, "modern" watercolour appears with Dürer in the 1490s and at once attains a zenith, in landscapes, townscapes and studies of plants, animals and costumes. With no direct heir in this field, Dürer links up across the centuries with Cézanne, and comparison of watercolours by these two with the late but still significant work of one of the Chinese literati painters, on the common theme of rocks and water touching the essence of landscape, shows the affinities and differences between the two traditions. Another comparison is offered between Bruegel and an earlier Chinese master, and still others could be made, for by its nature and content the watercolour is, of our techniques, the one that comes closest to Oriental art.

Dürer's magnificent watercolours remained an isolated achievement at that time. Leonardo, Bruegel and the painters of the Danube School, like Altdorfer and Wolf Huber, drew their spellbound landscapes in pen and ink, only adding watercolour exceptionally for delicate punctuations of colour. The Venetians, masters of colour and of the lyrical landscape, adopted for their drawings the famous blue paper tinted directly in the fibre and well suited to pictorial effects; but they did not practise watercolour painting. After the Reformation and the sack of Rome (1527), the sixteenth century came under the sway of Michelangelo and the Mannerist theoreticians whose one ideal model was the human body and its outline. Watercolour maintained itself in portraiture, popular imagery and the preparatory drawings for tapestries and decorative compositions, where some indication of colour was necessary; also in topographical art, botanical and ethnographic studies, and architectural and ornamental designs.

In the seventeenth century it reappeared in all its transparency and freshness with Van Dyck, who represents another landmark after Dürer: Van Dyck's stay in England was decisive both for the landscape and the portrait watercolour. The Dutch little masters practised it too. They were accomplished specialists, each in his own field; the charm and attractiveness of their colours ensured the success of their work. Avercamp's open-air watercolours and Adriaen van Ostade's rustic interiors were already considered as works of art in their own right.

In major painters like Poussin, Claude Lorrain and Rembrandt, the luminist vision favourable to landscape and the increasing practice of brush-wash drawing for such work led to an extraordinary development of the monochrome watercolour, which again has parallels with China.

The eighteenth century marks the return to colour and to a generalized use of drawing in its various forms as a fully autonomous means of expression recognized by art lovers and accepted at the Salons and exhibitions. Concurrently with other colour techniques like red chalk and pastel, watercolour was taken up widely in Europe, chiefly in France and at Venice, and for reasons often pointed out it became in England a typically national art, with its own statutes and societies. In France the terms "aquarelle" and "gouache," deriving from Italian, appeared in the artistic vocabulary in the 1770s and were then often confused, whereas in England the distinction was much sharper between watercolour on the one hand and gouache or bodycolour on the other. Thanks to the conjunction there of skilful practitioners, enthusiastic connoisseurs and outstanding mas-

Wen Chia
(1501-1583)
Landscape in the Spirit of
Verses by Tu Fu, 1576.
Ink and light colours.

Albrecht Dürer
(1471-1528)
The Quarry, c. 1495.
Watercolour.

ters like Turner, Blake and Constable, England launched the modern rise of watercolour painting, giving scope to all the new possibilities of the medium.

From this English source, the watercolour gained the Continent by way of France and spread to America. It answered to the spontaneity prized by the Romantics, to the cult of nature, to the obsession with dreamworlds and the East. It had its chroniclers and poets, its realists and visionaries. Few artists of the nineteenth century, major or minor, failed to try their hand at it, not to mention the legion of amateurs, and its resources were powerfully exploited according to their temperament by independent geniuses like Géricault and Daumier.

The pre-Impressionists Boudin and Jongkind were remarkable watercolourists, while the Impressionists themselves transferred to oil painting the limpidity of watercolour and its atmospheric magic. Cézanne turned to it in the deepening lyricism of his late work, and the revelation of his sublime watercolours was decisive for all the revolutionary movements that arose in the early twentieth century, Fauvism and Expressionism, Cubism and Futurism, and then abstraction.

With the use of collage and mixed media, and the intensive experimentation attending them, watercolour has lost its primacy in contemporary art. But some artists are still attracted by the harmonies and refinements it affords, and it remains a subtle and challenging medium for those who would sound the depths of the unconscious or, by a sifting and decanting, would hark back to the aesthetic of Far Eastern art.

Albrecht Dürer (1471-1528)
View of Arco, 1495. Watercolour and gouache.

10

Invention and Vocation of the Watercolour

1

The transition from the medieval illumination to the Renaissance drawing was made by way of the model books and sketchbooks used in artists' workshops as a repertory of designs, some of the leaves being heightened with colours. One of the best known model books is the one in the town library at Bergamo, attributed to the circle of Giovannino de' Grassi, a painter, architect and sculptor who worked in Milan on the cathedral and the castle of the Visconti from 1389 to 1398. Its thirty-one vellum leaves, delicately heightened with watercolour, contain drawings of plants, animals, emblems and female musicians characteristic of European court art. With Pisanello, one of the finest, most exquisite draughtsmen of all time, the ordinary studio pattern book was transformed into an experimental sketchbook, late Gothic stylization being combined in it with the naturalistic freshness of the early Renaissance. Working at the princely courts of Italy and heralding Leonardo in some ways, by his wandering life and his impassioned curiosity, Pisanello was fascinated, like de' Grassi, by the animal kingdom, but he also drew nudes, portraits, pageant ornaments and costumed figures, in pen and ink touched up with watercolour.

Of the thousand or so drawings left by Dürer, about sixty may be regarded as watercolours in various degrees: pen and ink sketches worked over with watercolours; watercolours of plants and animals extensively heightened with gouache; and almost pure watercolour landscapes handled with an unprecedented spontaneity and grasped, one feels, in their earthy essence. This last group, the most amazing of all, was made before and during his first journey to Venice (1494-1495), during which Dürer discovered the landscape backgrounds of Italian painting and the natural scenery of the Tyrol and the North Italian Alps. This body of work has always been of the keenest interest to connoisseurs, who have tried again and again to evaluate its scope and establish its chronological sequence. Four of these watercolours appear to pre-date his departure from Nuremberg; fifteen to record places he saw during the journey; and twelve to have been done shortly after his return to Nuremberg. The square sheet in the Louvre, the *View of Arco*, is the finest of the series, for the accurately defined relations between the structure of ground, vegetation and buildings, and the luminous atmosphere pervading them. Dürer omitted the mountain range on the horizon in order to focus on the rock fortress, carrying the eye up towards it through the vine and olive clad slopes and their shimmering colours. On his return home, he continued the series with some simple landscape motifs in the neighbourhood of Nuremberg, like the *Quarry* of pink sandstone overgrown with weeds and bushes, and the *Pond in the Woods* with its storm-lopped trees: here he achieved masterpieces prefiguring the Romantics and Cézanne.

Leonardo da Vinci felt the same wonder at the beauties of nature, but scrutinized them with a scientific eye. Both of these artists recorded an apocalyptic vision of the Deluge: Dürer after a terrifying dream in 1525, which on waking he set down in watercolour, showing masses of water pouring down from dark clouds, and adding underneath a written account of his vision; Leonardo, an expert in hydraulics, in the famous drawing of about 1515, also annotated, showing jets of water raining down from the sky and curling obsessively like locks of hair. Dürer's watercolours from nature are his boldest innovation, but there are no more of them after 1500, as Dürer turned to other preoccupations and other means of expression. The fascination with landscape then reappears, given a new and mysterious impetus, in the work of the Danube School—Altdorfer and Wolf Huber. Their intuitive and poetic approach to nature and its secret forces is akin to that of the contemporary philosopher Paracelsus, who was haunted by the same places. The humanistic Reformation and the example of Dürer also favoured the rise of portraiture. Watercolour and gouache were used by Cranach, Holbein and Manuel Deutsch for their preparatory portrait sketches from life. During his triumphal journey through the Netherlands (1520-1521) Dürer kept a written and illustrated journal of his movements. Most of his portrait drawings are in pen and silverpoint, but he also made some watercolour sketches of various subjects (Irish galloglasses, head of a stranded whale) and the so-called *Ladies of Livonia* in strange costumes.

Journeys for artistic, topographical or ethnographical purposes, with watercolour as the recording medium, became more numerous both in Europe and from Europe to distant lands. Between 1577 and 1590 John White took part in English expeditions to North America, and his watercolours published in the form of prints offer a valuable eyewitness record of Indian life and Eskimo types at that time.

Pieter Bruegel in turn made a journey to Italy by way of the Alps (1552-1554). He brought back a fine series of pen and ink drawings, some of them touched up with watercolour. Remarkable for their wealth of detail and the unity of the whole, they have that cosmic respiration and ordered patterning of mountains and valleys which brings to mind the old Chinese masters; and as with the latter, and unlike Leonardo and Dürer, the immense sweep of the landscape is punctuated with tiny figures.

Architectural and ornamental designs make up a distinct sector of watercolour painting. Before the modern cleavage between fine arts and applied arts, each major master commanded the whole register of creative work and design, from monuments to jewelry, and could provide models for craftsmen in any field. The Italian Mannerists, Perin del Vaga, Beccafumi, Lelio Orsi, Pordenone, and northern artists too like Tobias Stimmer or Hans Holbein in Switzerland and South Germany, drew in watercolour their projects for painted facades in the style of the period, with lively narrative scenes unfolding around architectural fantasies.

Giovannino de' Grassi
(active in Milan 1389-1398)

Two Women Making Music.
Pen and watercolour on vellum.

Pisanello
(c. 1395-c. 1455)

Costume Studies.
Pen and watercolour on vellum.

On his first, decisive journey to Venice in the autumn of 1494, Dürer painted some panoramas and urban scenes which were still of a topographical character. The major watercolour of Arco, in the Trentino district, done on his way home in 1495, is an accomplished example of classic balance between natural and architectural elements. In the melancholy landscape with a pond, near Nuremberg, datable to 1495-1497, human constructions have disappeared and nature stands alone, offering her simplest motifs: the blue sweep of the pond in the foreground, delicately fringed with sedge; the sparse clump of trees on one side, shorn of their tops by a storm; on the other, the lighter stretch of the dune and a grove of leafy trees; beyond, the setting sun glowing through orange and lilac clouds. Here Dürer shows his mastery of transparent, blended colours, his romantic response to the movements

and nuances of atmosphere. The sketch-like handling of this watercolour adds to its suggestive power and modern resonance.

A burgher of Regensburg in Bavaria, Altdorfer visited Austria several times to carry out religious paintings, and like Cranach, whose influence marks his early work, he responded to the peculiar charm of the region. During the 1520s landscape apprehended in its animistic power occupies a central place in Altdorfer's paintings and drawings, both remarkable for their intense expressiveness. To that period belongs this mountain landscape, in pen and watercolour, traversed vertically by the trunk of a pine tree, a common compositional device. Deep in the valley stands the village with its mountain stream, its church tower, its hilltop castle: around them the artist has set out the real and imaginary elements of a mood-creating poetry.

Albrecht Dürer
(1471-1528)
Pond in the Woods, c. 1495-1497.
Watercolour and gouache.

Albrecht Altdorfer
(c. 1480-1538)
Mountain Landscape with Stream
and Village, c. 1520-1530.
Pen and watercolour.

15

Leonardo da Vinci
(1452-1519)
Gigantic Explosion, c. 1515.
Black chalk and ink wash.

Albrecht Dürer
(1471-1528)
Dream Vision (Landscape Flooded
with Waters from Heaven), 1525.
Pen and watercolour.

Tung Yüan
(907-960)
Clear Weather in the Valley.
Ink and light colours on paper.

Pieter Bruegel the Elder
(c. 1525-1569)

Mountain Landscape with
Monastery, 1552.
Pen and watercolour.

◄ Niklaus Manuel Deutsch
(1484-1530)

Portrait of a Young Woman in Profile, c. 1529.
Coloured chalks and watercolour.

Hans Holbein the Younger
(1497/98-1543)

Design for the Façade Decoration
of the Haus zum Tanz in the
Eisengasse, Basel, 1520-1522.
Pen and watercolour.

Albrecht Dürer
(1471-1528)
Ladies of Livonia, 1521.
Pen and watercolour.

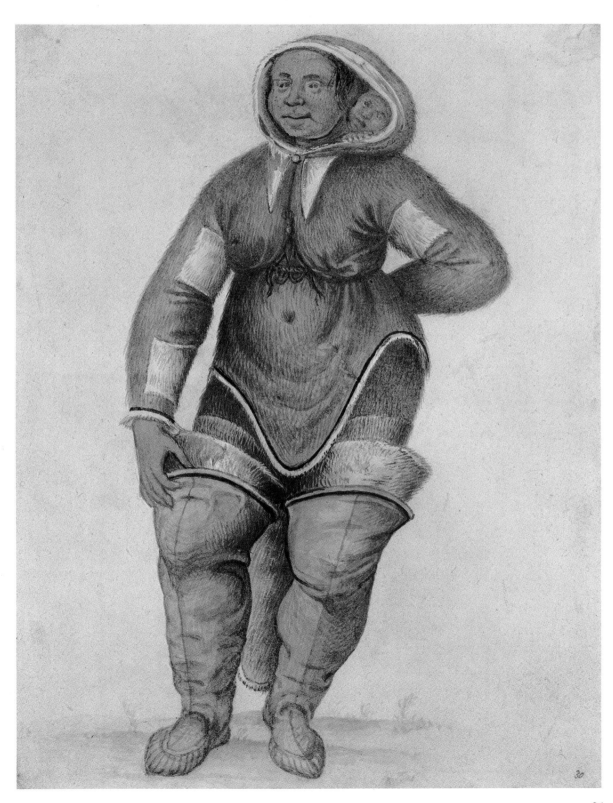

John White
(active 1577-1590)
Eskimo Woman, 1585-1590.
Watercolour touched with white.

Albrecht Dürer
(1471-1528)
The Great Piece of Turf, 1503.
Watercolour and gouache.

Botany and Natural Sciences

2

In China the painting of flowers, birds and animals was an old subject category going back to the T'ang period (A.D.618-906). It blossomed under the Sung dynasty (960-1279), one of whose emperors was himself an eminent bird and flower painter. These subjects had to be done from life, and indeed the Chinese described them as "life writing." This kind of painting did not appear in Europe till the fifteenth century, in the form of coloured drawings. Watercolour was well suited to this kind of work, and here again the decisive impetus came from Dürer. Technically, his pictures of the animal and vegetable kingdoms form a distinct group. Unlike his landscapes, they are not watercolours in the strict sense, for over the transparent undercoats he applied strokes of opaque gouache with a stiff brush to fix the linear patterns firmly. This complex procedure, combining the easy flow of colours with precision of line, answered to his need to record visible nature down to its smallest details.

In a pen and watercolour composition at the Albertina in Vienna, Dürer brought together in a joyous garland around the Virgin all the beasts and plants that he had been depicting separately. The *Sea Crab* (Boymans-van Beuningen Museum, Rotterdam), assigned to his first stay in Venice in 1495, and the *Hare* (Albertina, Vienna), monogrammed and dated 1502, number among his finest animal studies, remarkable for their evocative power and hallucinating fidelity to nature. Each is recorded as a singular entity and as an emblem of the species. In his still lifes of birds hanging by the beak like hunting trophies, the rendering of plumage and down is a prodigy of accuracy and fine colour shadings; they point the way to Cranach's splendid version of the same theme in the Dresden Museum.

Dürer's studies of flowers and plants, datable to 1502-1505, just before his second journey to Venice, culminated in the *Great Piece of Turf* (Albertina, Vienna), expressly dated 1503. This heavy clod, cut from the still damp earth and scrutinized intensely with the weeds and plant life growing out of it, raises the density of the microcosm to the power of the macrocosm, for the circulation of life is universal and the principle of correspondence between the whole and its parts governs creation. Art has *to be extracted* from nature, wrote Dürer, and mastery is even better revealed in the smaller than in the greater things.

With these unsurpassed watercolours Dürer inaugurated the painting of botany and natural history, a hybrid genre in which artistic standards were to be long maintained without detriment to scientific requirements. After a youthful voyage to Florida, Jacques Le Moyne de Morgues, exiled from France as a Protestant, settled in London in 1581. There he became one of the first to record the flora of England, and the publisher who issued prints of his flower watercolours, which Le Moyne meant to be "right and accurate," also issued those of John White. At the same period, working in this same field of botany, the Flemish painter and miniaturist Georg Hoefnagel met with great success in Vienna and Central Europe. In the Netherlands, where flower growing was a national passion and the still life an independent and popular genre, pictures of flowers, fruit, butterflies, insects and shells—initiated by two immigrant Flemish artists, Jacob de Gheyn and Ambrosius Bosschaert—were much in demand during the classical period and found a numerous clientele among owners of those art and curio cabinets so characteristic of the age. The still life by the Delft painter Balthasar van der Ast (p. 25) brings together animal and vegetable elements to realistic effect, with symbolic implications, and his prominent signature speaks for the recognition now given to the watercolour technique. The naturalistic tradition was continued in Holland in the eighteenth century with the division between fruit and flower painters, like Jan van Huysum, and bird and animal painters, like Aert Schouman.

Maria Sibylla Merian inherited from her father—the Frankfurt engraver Matthäus Merian—and transmitted to her children the taste for drawing and the natural sciences. She depicted both flowers and insects, which she studied in Germany and Holland. Her venturesome passion for entomology took her to Dutch Guinea, where her range and gifts were further developed. There, with scientific accuracy and in a style of her own, she painted some astonishing watercolours of tropical birds and reptiles.

In France the brother of Louis XIII, Gaston d'Orléans, created an important botanical garden at Blois. He called in the best flower painters available, who painted their delicate watercolours on the smooth, supple ground of vellum sheets. At his death in 1660, his picture collections were bequeathed to his nephew Louis XIV and thereafter continually added to, amounting in the end to five hundred volumes of vellum sheets now preserved in the Muséum d'Histoire Naturelle, Paris. Of the eighty artists commissioned up to 1907 to draw plant life in collaboration with the botanists of the Jardin des Plantes in Paris, several stand out for their brilliant artistic qualities combined with the highest standard of accuracy. Nicolas Robert, already recruited by Gaston d'Orléans, and Claude Aubriet, travelling companion of the famous botanist Tournefort in the Levant (1700-1702), still belong to the glorious reign of Louis XIV. The most gifted member of a family of naturalist painters and decorators, Pierre Joseph Redouté is best known for his large watercolours of lilies and roses; he also painted some separate sheets of fruits, which are no less remarkable. Born in the Antilles and brought up in Paris, where as a boy he attended David's classes, John James Audubon settled in the United States at eighteen and devoted himself to ornithology. His precise and systematic watercolours of birds, seen in close-up in their natural habitat, have a real artistic value by virtue of their strong colours and telling design.

Lucas Cranach the Elder
(1472-1553)
Two Birds Hanging from a Nail, c. 1530.
Watercolour and gouache.

24

Balthasar van der Ast
(1593/94-1656/57)
Still Life with Shells,
Plums and Cherries.
Pen and watercolour.

The amazingly truthful still life by Cranach the Elder followed up similar studies by Dürer of birds hanging by the beak. Their common prototype is the famous *Partridge* (Alte Pinakothek, Munich) painted in trompe-l'œil in 1504, on a wooden panel, by the Venetian master Jacopo de Barbari during a stay in Germany, and deriving in turn from Italian inlaid work. The watercolour technique with gouache heightening permitted an accurate rendering of the finest shades of colour in feathers and down, and a flawless combination of artistic excellence and naturalistic fidelity.

Flower painting, originating in Italy and brilliantly illustrated in Germany by Dürer, was developed in the Netherlands during the latter half of the sixteenth century as a local speciality of both artistic and scientific interest. It appealed to art lovers and curio collectors, to botanists and horticulturists, to publishers of herbals and natural history books. The artists who turned to this genre, whose exacting detail called for watercolour, were mostly Flemish émigrés: Georg Hoefnagel in Central Europe, where he worked at the imperial court in Vienna and for Rudolf II in Prague; Jacob de Gheyn and Ambrosius Bosschaert in the northern Netherlands, where they established the Dutch type of flower piece. Bosschaert's pupil and brother-in-law, Balthasar van der Ast, continued his limpid manner and archaic layout, first at Utrecht, then at Delft. The signed watercolour in the British Museum is an example of his assortments of choice objects and his careful technique, under an even play of transparent light. The symbolism of the old Vanitas still life is not ruled out by his naturalistic precision. The fragility of the leaves and fruit (plums and cherries), at the mercy of various insects (flies, bees, dragon-flies), is contrasted with the mineral toughness of exotic shells of various shapes. Another version of this picture, painted on metal, is dated 1628. One of Van der Ast's pupils was Jan Davidsz de Heem, and his influence was still strong on Jan van Huysum, the most admired fruit and flower painter of the eighteenth century, who was equally at home in watercolours and oils.

25

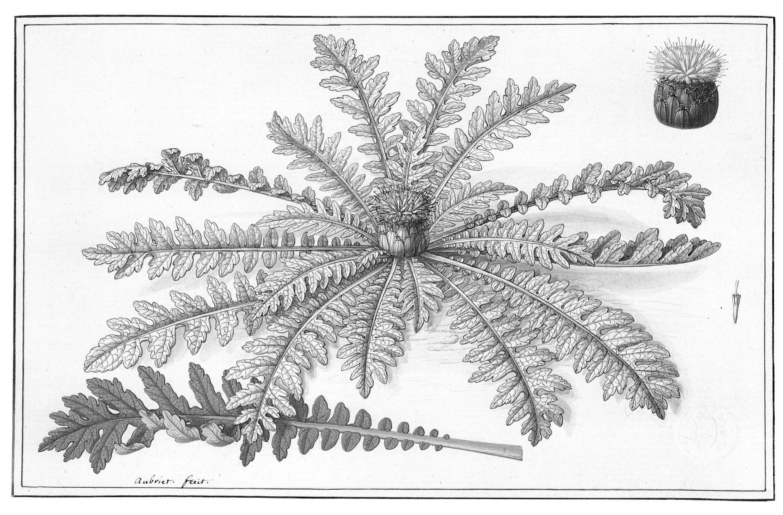

Claude Aubriet
(c. 1665-1742)
Cinara Africana.
Pen and watercolour.

Born at Châlons-sur-Marne about 1665 and appointed "peintre du roy, de son Cabinet et du Jardin du roy" on 23 January 1700, as the successor of Nicolas Robert and Jean Joubert, Claude Aubriet was the third and last of the painter-naturalists in the service of Louis XIV. He was trained by the famous botanist Tournefort, whose scientific works he illustrated and whom he accompanied on his journey to the Levant (1700-1702): there, working side by side with Tournefort, he made many drawings and watercolours of eastern plants, later reproduced on vellum.

Apart from this journey, Aubriet's professional life was spent between the Jardin des Plantes in Paris, where he was provided with lodgings, and the Ménagerie de Versailles, where he went to draw the rare birds and animals. He also made an extensive series of studies of butterflies for a book on insects and their changing forms which was never published.

In 1699 the intrepid Maria Sibylla Merian sailed with her daughter Dorothea, also a painter, for the Dutch colony of Surinam in South America. There she spent two years. She was a gifted entomologist and the result of her visit was a set of sixty plates engraved after her watercolour studies of insect life at Surinam (this in addition to her previous studies of European insects). Her scientific curiosity also extended to the local flora and fauna. She was fascinated by the dramatic clashes between reptiles and birds, and the elegance of her curvilinear style was on a par with her accuracy. Here the snake has coiled itself round the heron, and the shadow of its body is cast over the plumage of the bird.

John James Audubon
(1785-1851)
Purple Grackle, 1822.
Watercolour.

Pierre Joseph Redouté ▶
(1759-1840)
Fruit, 1834.
Watercolour.

In a report of 1838 to the Académie des Sciences in Paris, the naturalist Cuvier wrote: "Among the fine works which in various countries have been devoted to representing the productions of nature, there are none which, for the finish of the engraving and colouring, surpass the one that Monsieur Audubon is publishing on the birds of North America, and there is not one that equals it for the size of the plates." The latter were then being printed in England (1827-1838) from Audubon's original watercolours.

Pierre Joseph Redouté was the flower painter first of Queen Marie-Antoinette at the Trianon, then of the Empress Joséphine at Malmaison. He illustrated various works on botany and added some new pieces to the historic collection of plant pictures on vellum at the Muséum d'Histoire Naturelle in Paris, where he was appointed drawing master in 1823. His watercolour drawings of fruit are much rarer than, but just as fine as, the sets of flower watercolours for which he is so famous.

Sir Anthony Van Dyck
(1599-1641)
Landscape.
Watercolour.

The Luminist Vision

3

While Italian art lovers and theorists claimed supremacy for their country in figure painting, they at once recognized landscape as a new and valid category and a northern speciality. In his *Schilderboek* (1604) Karel van Mander, the Dutch Vasari, confirms this polarity from the Dutch point of view: "One finds that on the whole the painters of our country have a marked preference for landscape. They have, at the very least, proved skilful in this genre which goes against the grain of the Italians, whom everyone calls skilful landscapists but who describe themselves as masters in the art of figures."

Something has been said about the decisive contribution made to landscape by Dürer and the Germanic lands, and by Bruegel and the still united Low Countries before they were divided between the Northern and Southern provinces. It is fascinating to follow the transition between Mannerism, with its Europe-wide formulas, and the two local schools in the Netherlands. The growing distinction between the latter, one decorative and baroque, the other realistic and intimate, opened a phase of intense graphic activity. The transition was made by several Flemish landscapists who, after working in Italy, returned and stayed home, like Joost de Momper, or sought refuge in Holland, like Gillis van Coninxloo and Roelandt Savery. Before settling in Amsterdam, where one of his many pupils was the extraordinary etcher Hercules Seghers, Coninxloo joined for a few years the Rhenish art colony at Frankenthal, a crossroads of Venetian, Germanic and northern trends. Rudolf II in Prague, a fabulous collector who owned watercolours by Dürer and landscapes by Bruegel, and gathered around him a cosmopolitan circle of artists and scientists, commissioned Roelandt Savery to draw the animals in his zoo and to travel through the Tyrol, sketching the wild mountain scenery and picturesque sites. Trained in Antwerp and working in Paris, where he was ennobled by Louis XIII, Jacques Fouquières is a talented representative of the Franco-Flemish approach to landscape. Under Louis XIV, the Brussels painter Frans van der Meulen was employed as a landscapist at the Gobelins tapestry works; and as "painter of the king's conquests" he accompanied Louis XIV on his military campaigns. From Meulen's drawings, heightened with watercolour, Israël Silvestre of Nancy made the prints composing the topographical repertory of France.

Rubens, like Titian, did his finest studies of trees and nature in black chalk, but his oil sketches on paper have the spontaneity of watercolours. His two brilliant collaborators, Van Dyck and Jordaens, soon struck out on paths of their own and both liked to heighten their preparatory drawings with watercolour, especially when these were tapestry designs. Though best known as a portraitist, Van Dyck made many landscape sketches in the various places where he lived, and at least four sheets of his final English period again achieve, by a brief miracle, the freshness of pure watercolour, unseen since Dürer, with fluid and radiant colours set off by the white unpainted areas of the paper.

Caravaggio and Vermeer and the virtuosos of the Golden Century, Frans Hals and Velazquez, made no drawings, because they drew as they painted, following the Venetian example of Giorgione. Line with them was no longer a preliminary design but rather an integral part, at every stage, of the picture's steady build-up and of its creative dynamism. Rubens and Rembrandt, Poussin and Claude Lorrain, symmetrical pairs of opposing and complementary temperaments, all practised drawing indefatigably, both for its own sake and for the purposes of their oil paintings. At once classical and baroque, the painting of the seventeeth century was essentially tonal, governed by the principle of values. It was based on the luminist vision attuned to the development of landscape and the expression of feelings. The pictorial form substituted for the plastic form led in the field of drawing to the generalized use of the ink and brush technique and the flexible practice of wash drawing with infinite modulations; and such washes may well be described as monochrome watercolours. Claude and Poussin recorded the ideal light and solemn sweep of the Roman Campagna; Rembrandt and Ruisdael, the natural light and atmospheric respiration of the Dutch plain, steeped in their own sense of religious awe. This was the grave and noble moment of Western landscape painting, when space was still a unity rich in spiritual overtones.

The two focal points of landscape painting were then the Roman Campagna, imbued with its age-old harmony, and the hybrid earth of Holland won back by man from the sea and giving rise to its own native style. Rome was then the international art centre, and there, before Claude and Poussin, came the northern artists who initiated the renewal of landscape: the Fleming Paul Bril, in an elegiac mood, and the German Adam Elsheimer, in a more intensely poetic mood reaching back to Altdorfer and the Venetians. Draughtsmen as much as painters, both of them had that innate sense of light, the soul of landscape, which was lacking in even the most gifted Italians, like the Carracci, whose skilfully contrived lighting remains artificial. Poussin in his figure paintings refers back to the Italians; in his landscape drawings he looks rather to northern examples, vying here with Claude and transposing them into his personal idiom. Elsheimer came from Frankfurt, the home ground of the Merian family, where watercolour was practised by Georg Flegel, a painter of natural history, and by Wenzel Hollar, who drew and engraved urban views.

Like Claude and Poussin, the great Dutch landscapists kept, in their drawings from nature, to tonal monochrome and the aerial resources of wash drawing. Watercolour was practised rather by artists on the fringe of the national tradition, like Pieter Berchem in his Italian landscapes on pastoral themes or Allart van Everdingen in his Scandinavian views of waterfalls and rocky coasts; also by Philips Koninck, a painter much admired by Van Gogh, to punctuate with colour his panoramic views of rivers, dunes and hills. It was used with brio and accuracy by those typically Dutch genre painters, Hendrik Avercamp in his open-air scenes and Adriaen van Ostade in his interiors with carousing or brawling peasants; also by the architectural painter Pieter Saenredam for the measured heightening of his crystalline church interiors.

Roelandt Savery
(1576-1639)

Mountain Landscape.
Pen, bistre and watercolour.

Jacques Fouquières ▶
(c. 1590-1659)

Stream in the Woods.
Watercolour and gouache.

Nicolas Poussin
(1594-1665)
View of the Aventine in Rome, c. 1645.
Black chalk and bistre wash.

Claude Lorrain
(1600-1682)
View of the Tiber from Monte Mario, c. 1640.
Brush and brown wash.

Rembrandt
(1606-1669)

View on the Bullewijk, looking
towards Ouderkerk, with a
Rowing Boat, c. 1650.
Pen and brown wash,
touched with bodycolour.

Philips Koninck
(1619-1688)

Bird's Eye View of a
River Landscape.
Pen, bistre, watercolour,
with touches of bodycolour.

Hendrik Avercamp
(1585-1634)
Canal with Sailing Boats near Amsterdam.
Pen and bistre, and watercolour.

Hendrik Avercamp, known as the "Mute of Kampen" because of a natural infirmity, was trained in Amsterdam by immigrant Flemish painters of the Mannerist school. He reduced their exuberant fancy to the realist standard of Dutch taste, to the naïve and colloquial pungency of his personal vision. He liked winter scenes and landscapes animated by ice skaters, and riverscapes with quiet anglers among passing boats. The bright touches of colour applied to costumes go to set off the delicate blond monochrome of the whole. He made drawings on the same themes, often heightened with watercolour; atmosphere is rendered with even greater delicacy, and they were much sought after.

Architectural painting was one of the most distinct and characteristic branches of Dutch art, with set types of exteriors and in-

teriors. One of its initiators was Pieter Saenredam, a native of Ass-
endelft, who spent most of his life at Haarlem. He had a sound
technical knowledge acquired from schooling with architects.
The purity of his bare, transparent forms makes him the most at-
tractive master of this genre. Between 1628 and 1665 he visited
the principal towns of Holland, painting historic monuments and
church interiors from drawings made on the spot, punctuated with
watercolour and often dated to the month and year (here May
1661). He worked with unfailing accuracy, showing a profound
comprehension of internal structures and a sensitive response to
space and colour (usually in tonalities of grey and pink), to the
silent, mellow play of light, to the nostalgic modulation of time
under the great stone vaults.

Pieter Saenredam
(1597-1665)
Interior of the Groote Kerk at Alkmaar,
looking towards the Organ, 1661.
Pen and bistre, washed with
Indian ink and watercoloured.

Thomas Gainsborough
(1727-1788)
Wooded Landscape with Wagon
in a Glade, mid-1760s.
Black chalk and watercolour
heightened with white.

England and Europe in the Eighteenth Century

4

After the phase of tonal painting and monochrome wash, colour came to the fore in the eighteenth century, from the simple vignette to the monumental decoration, being taken up in all the drawing techniques then in popular use—red chalk, pastel, three-crayon, gouache, watercolour. The word watercolour occurs already in Shakespeare (*1 Henry IV*, v.i.80) and watercolour drawings appear in England in the sixteenth century, for studies of plants, topography, and American scenery and natives. But the real incunabula of the medium, both artistically and technically, were Van Dyck's delightful watercolours, as isolated an achievement in their time as Dürer's had been. The flowering of watercolour painting in England after 1750 became, for over a century, a national phenomenon, peculiarly insular in character, but originating on the Continent.

In a country whose empirical philosophy was based on the primacy of sensations, whose parks and gardens retained the wild beauties of the countryside, whose clouds were eagerly studied both by scientists and by poets and painters, whose aesthetic thought laid down the categories of the sublime and the picturesque as corresponding to two subjective responses to the grandiose or intimate sides of nature—there, in England, appeared a new conception of landscape, an atmospheric vision of the natural world that watercolour was best suited to rendering in all its delicate hues. English art lovers collected earlier landscape painting, in particular the lyrical landscapes of Claude Lorrain; and they welcomed and patronized the new Venetian painters who looked to nature, like Marco Ricci and Francesco Zuccarelli, whose light-toned gouaches were much appreciated, and Canaletto, who cast the glow of Venetian light over his views of the Thames and the neighbourhood of London. Canaletto left his mark on the English landscape, which by now had its own practitioners, such as Richard Wilson, active in Wales and Italy, whose talent and pioneering role were recognized by Ruskin, and Thomas Gainsborough, who painted his portraits to order and his landscapes for pleasure. The latter's radiant watercolours of the Bath period embody the essence of the picturesque as defined by Gainsborough's theorist-friends.

The initiator of the English watercolour was Paul Sandby, who began as draughtsman to the Military Drawing Office of the Tower of London, then to the Military Survey in Scotland. Out of a long topographical tradition he grew and matured. He never travelled abroad and worked for years on favourite themes in Windsor Park, where his brother Thomas was Deputy Ranger, and in the rustic neighbourhood of his house in Bayswater. Bodycolour he used eclectically in idealized scenes, watercolour in the realistic and familiar views that represent his finest work. Figures are harmoniously integrated into his landscapes, which combine architecture and nature with an unfailing mastery of perspective. Alexander Cozens, who devised a method of composing landscapes from "blots," kept to the wash, but his son John Robert Cozens painted large watercolours imbued with the majestic,

melancholy impressions felt at twilight in the Alps or on the Italian lakes. In the 1790s, when his mind had given way, John Robert Cozens was looked after by Dr. Thomas Monro, an art patron and amateur watercolourist whose house in Adelphi Terrace was open to young artists, among them Girtin and Turner, who there schooled themselves by copying some of Cozens' luminous, poetic watercolours. Thomas Girtin never saw the Alps or visited Italy. His career was short but influential. Like the true creator he was, he assimilated the lesson of his elders and transmuted it in accordance with his temperament. His range includes both urban scenes and country views whose most prominent feature is the sky. His warm tonality dominated by ochre and brown contrasts with the cool, bluish colour scale of Cozens. With Girtin opens a new age of watercolour: he gave it its technical freedom and autonomy, achieving a fusion between form, colour and light.

In France three of the greatest painters of the eighteenth century, Watteau, Boucher and Chardin, ignored the watercolour medium. It was practised by many little masters versed in illustration and ornamentation, designers of pageantry, stage scenery and *scènes galantes*—Eisen, Cochin, Baudouin, Huet, Debucourt, Pillement, Carmontelle, Mallet, Challes, Hoin, Leprince and so on. Another was Gabriel de Saint-Aubin, a lively, colour-loving artist, who never went anywhere without pencil and sketchbook and stands out as a chronicler of Parisian life, where open-air exhibitions and auction sales were becoming more numerous. Close friends of the same age, with a common background of Italian travel and sightseeing excursions with the Abbé de Saint-Non, Hubert Robert and Jean-Honoré Fragonard both handled red chalk, wash and watercolour with easy mastery and composed their Rococo genre scenes and Neo-classical landscapes in a vein of pre-Romantic sensibility. For his publications illustrated with prints, the Abbé de Saint-Non recruited other draughtsmen too, like L.J. Desprez, who was later patronized by the king of Sweden. Jean Houël sold five hundred of his delicate watercolours to Catherine the Great of Russia, to finance the publication of his set of views of Sicily and Malta. Louis-Gabriel Moreau the Elder, in his views of the countryside around Paris, carried on the French landscape tradition running from Fouquet to Corot, and did so with a personal accent comparable to that of the English watercolourists. Rome was the international art centre and the picturesque place above all others. There watercolourists from all over Europe met and vied with each other, among them the then famous German artist Philipp Hackert, whose biography was written by Goethe. Switzerland, whose lake and Alpine scenery was attracting more and more artists, had its own watercolourists: J.L. Aberli, who kept to his native Bernese Alps; Louis Ducros, patronized by English collectors during his stay in Rome; and S.H. Grimm, who settled in London. In Venice Francesco Guardi condensed, with a vibrancy of his own, the light and life of the lagoon. Finally, the picturesque and humorous side of social life was recorded by Thomas Rowlandson in England and Cornelius Troost in Holland.

Paul Sandby
(1730-1809)
The Artist's Studio, 4 St George's Row,
Bayswater, c. 1800.
Watercolour and bodycolour
on blue paper.

John Robert Cozens
(1752-1797)
Between Sallanches and Servoz,
Mont Blanc in the Distance, 1776.
Watercolour.

Living in London from 1776 till his death in 1809, Paul Sandby occupied a house (demolished in 1901) overlooking Hyde Park, in the then still rural neighbourhood of Bayswater. Thomas Girtin lived nearby for several months. Sandby's studio stood on a terrace surrounded by gardens.

John Robert Cozens' view of the Alps, with Mont Blanc rising through mist and clouds in the distance, is dated 27 August 1776: it was made as he passed through Savoy on his first journey to Italy, with the collector and critic Richard Payne Knight, who owned a fine group of drawings by Claude Lorrain. The tiny figures on the riverbank, in the foreground, indicate the scale and emphasize the grand sweep of this Alpine view. The underdrawing that still governs the work of Cozens and Sandby is done away with in Girtin's magnificent watercolour.

Francesco Guardi
(1712-1793)
Sketch for a Ceiling Decoration.
Sepia, brown wash and watercolour.

Unlike most of the Venetian painters of his time, who were invited to England, Austria and Spain, Francesco Guardi never left home, but his suggestive, impressionistic pictures were just as much sought after by foreign collectors. His drawings are mostly views and capriccios in pen and ink, with small vibrant touches of wash; he also left some decorative designs heightened with watercolour. The Venetian painters from Veronese to Tiepolo were famous for their aerial ceiling frescoes on allegorical themes, which they carried into Central Europe. Guardi's watercolour design is for a Rococo ceiling painting surrounded by stucco decorations; further drawings for it are in the Museo Correr, Venice, and the City Museum, Plymouth (Devon). In the luminous oval of the sky, surrounded by scrolls and festoons, appear a female figure with billowing garments and two winged Cupids, one holding a bird with a cord—a symbol of love in thrall. This watercolour, remarkable for its quivering vitality, is no doubt a late work.

A highly gifted artist, Gabriel de Saint-Aubin led the life of an independent eccentric. Moved by a passion for drawing and an eager curiosity, he strolled through Paris noting down in his sketchbooks (three of which are preserved) the sights and scenes that met his eye in the streets. On 12 April 1778 he attended a performance in honour of Voltaire at the Théâtre-Français. Preceded by two sketches, this watercolour shows the audience giving an enthusiastic ovation to the old writer and looking towards the box where he was being crowned with laurels after the sixth performance of his last play, the verse tragedy *Irene* (Voltaire died just two months later). The architecture of the theatre, the silhouettes of the audience and the animation of the whole scene are marvellously rendered by the spirited linework and touches of colour. Saint-Aubin also produced a fine series of etchings in several states, many of them heightened with wash, watercolour or gouache.

Gabriel de Saint-Aubin
(1724-1780)

The Crowning of Voltaire at
the Théâtre-Français, Paris, 1778.
Watercolour.

Louis-Gabriel Moreau
(1739-1805)
View of the Château de Valençay,
1792.
Watercolour and gouache.

Jean Hoüel
(1735-1813)
The Greek Theatre at Syracuse,
1776-1779.
Watercolour and gouache.

44

Louis-Gabriel Moreau's landscapes usually represent the plains and hillsides of the Ile-de-France, but in 1792 he painted two companion views of the Château de Valençay (Indre), built in the sixteenth century and purchased in 1805 by Talleyrand. This view, from beneath the walls and terraces, is focused on the broad flight of steps (demolished soon afterwards). Both vegetation and architecture are pervaded by the clear light of spring; in the foreground the gardeners are at work, a rustic scene much to this painter's taste.

Jean Hoüel published a *Voyage pittoresque des isles de Sicile, de Malte et de Lipari* (1782-1787) in four volumes illustrated with 264 engravings from drawings he had made on the spot between 1776 and 1779. This watercolour of the Greek theatre at Syracuse is remarkable for the supple use of the medium, the freshness of the colours, the accuracy and simplicity with which light is recorded. The archaeological site, excavated by the painter himself, is absorbed into the rural landscape.

With Hubert Robert, on the contrary, the shattered remains of ancient ruins are grouped arbitrarily and prevail over nature. This large, carefully finished watercolour, dated 1786, was exhibited in Paris at the 1787 Salon as belonging to the Comtesse d'Angiviller, wife of the Superintendent of Royal Buildings, who promoted the Neo-classical aesthetic and the cult of antiquity. In the Louvre are two further Hubert Robert watercolours on a similar theme, but less finished than this one. Here, around the bas-relief from the Arch of Titus representing "Titus crowned by Victory," stand the helmeted statue of Athena and a headless statue of the "Dacian Prisoner." Two elegant young ladies are busily sketching in the open air amidst the ancient stones. These two figures vouch for the popularity of watercolour in eighteenth-century France, practised at court by the queen herself and by society ladies, and for the melancholy fascination of ruins—monuments midway between manmade works and nature, between the lingering past and the fleeting present.

Joseph Mallord William Turner
(1775-1851)
Venice, San Giorgio Maggiore from the Dogana, 1819.
Watercolour.

46

Romantic Landscape

5

While classicism reposes on the harmony of the human body and its well defined contours, romanticism looks to the boundless world of nature and the emotions it arouses. The term "romantic" was first applied, significantly enough, to landscapes: "The word designates landscapes which bring to mind the descriptions in romances" (dictionary of the French Academy, 1798). Even more than the novel, then assuming its modern form, English poetry from the time of Thomson's *Seasons* (1726-1730) took inspiration from nature, and the publication in 1798 of *Lyrical Ballads* by Wordsworth and Coleridge—one of whom was to be associated with Constable, the other with Turner—marks the birth of romanticism in literature and coincides with the rise of watercolour in painting.

Francis Towne is one of the early watercolourists of mountain scenery, built up by synthetic colour planes and incisive lines gradually developing from the sublime to the romantic. Turner, in the summer of 1802, made his first journey to the Continent to see the paintings accumulated in the Louvre by Napoleon and to visit Switzerland, where he in his turn tackled the Alpine themes of Cozens and Towne. Constable, who like Gainsborough remained at home, assumed the artistic and moral position, so difficult to maintain, of a "natural painter" (as Corot was to assume it later), for whom the simplest motif has its beauty, if bathed in light and seen by eager eyes. Constable painted his oil sketches on the spot, in the open air, and turned to watercolours only twice, in 1806 during his tour of the Lake District and after 1830 when he decided to exhibit his splendid watercolours regularly at the Royal Academy. Turner, on the contrary, made a continuous practice of watercolour painting, both realistic and visionary—for him an apt medium for systematic experimentation with the expressive properties of colour and light. Out of his almost yearly journeys through Britain and his travels on the Continent came a prodigious ensemble of twenty thousand drawings and watercolours, ranging from topographical studies to abstract variations. His first visit to Venice, in 1819, speeded up his inclination towards atmospheric phantasmagorias. Like Turner and Girtin, John Sell Cotman was patronized by Dr. Monro and worked in this collector's house in Adelphi Terrace. In Yorkshire he found his personal style, in terms of geometric structures and uniform areas of wash. Ruskin, who so much admired Turner, ignored Cotman.

Watercolourists as such not being admitted to the Royal Academy exhibitions, they founded their own professional societies in 1804 and 1807. One of the most influential members, through his zeal as a theorist and teacher, was John Varley, whose best pupil was David Cox, also a notable theorist and teacher. Peter De Wint, who also received counsel from Varley, painted landscapes and still lifes in velvety colours. Artistic relations between France and England were knit closer by the Romantic Salon of 1824, where Constable and Bonington created a sensation. The latter—who died of consumption at twenty-six—was initiated into watercolour at Calais, where he lived as a teenage boy, by Louis Francia who had been schooled by Girtin. In Paris from 1819, Bonington worked in the studio of Baron Gros, who encouraged and stimulated him. Bonington was the most gifted of the many English watercolourists who popularized their medium on the Continent, painting the beauties of Normandy and the picturesque course of the Seine. Delacroix, an anglophile and fond of watercolour, shared a Paris studio in 1824 with the English watercolourist Thales Fielding. In the summer of 1825 Delacroix visited England, where Géricault had preceded him (and had also tried his hand at watercolour), and where he fell in with Bonington and a whole colony of French painters. Returning to Paris with Bonington, Delacroix put him up for several months in his studio, and later acknowledged his technical debt to this charming friend and admirable artist whose watercolours, he said, "sparkled like diamonds." Bonington achieved the full mastery of his medium in 1826, the year of his journey to Italy. He treated the same subjects, seascape, landscape, genre and history, in a small format, as both oil painter and watercolourist, contriving to give his watercolours, without any loss of freshness, the density of oils, and his small oils the transparency and glow of watercolours. The French Romantic landscapists, Paul Huet and Eugène Isabey, his fellow students in Gros's studio, came under Bonington's influence as watercolourists. Auguste Ravier, working chiefly in his native region around Lyons, vied with Turner in the ardour of his colour harmonies. François-Marius Granet, a pupil of David and companion of Ingres in Rome, achieved in his late watercolours at Versailles something of the melancholy poetry of C. D. Friedrich, without the latter's allegories.

Of the same generation as Constable and Turner, Caspar David Friedrich is the greatest and most mysterious of the German Romantic landscapists. He settled in Dresden, a centre of art and culture, became friends with the painters Runge and Carus, and maintained relations with the poets Tieck, Kleist and Novalis. Friedrich drew inspiration from realistic motifs observed in the Harz mountains and on the shores of the Baltic; but on nature, indifferent to the oppressive sentiments it engenders, he conferred a sovereign silence of his own and his transcendental symbolism. The almost ascetic purity of form adds to the power of emotion and the strangeness of the light. His drawings in sepia wash, replacing bistre wash, are composite and spiritualistic landscapes, while his oils and watercolours are direct studies from nature. Karl Rottmann, a disciple of the pioneer J. A. Koch, brought back to Munich some lively watercolours from Italy and Greece, but failed in his attempts to transpose them into large-scale frescoes. In Berlin, marked by his journey to Italy and the shock of Turner, Karl Blechen adopted a free and colourful style which was carried on by Adolf Menzel. The Viennese master Thomas Ender brought home a series of delicately romantic watercolours from his expedition to Brazil in 1817 and then aligned himself on the placid and fruitful naturalism of Rudolf von Alt, who devoted his long life to the almost exclusive practice of watercolour.

48

Francis Towne
(1739 or 1740-1816)
The Source of the Arveiron, 1781.
Watercolour.

Joseph Mallord William Turner
(1775-1851)
The Source of the Arveiron, c. 1806-1809.
Watercolour and scraping-out over pencil.

Francis Towne's large watercolour is painted on four sheets pasted together (a smaller version on two superimposed sheets is in a private collection in London). On the back are annotations recording the site in the Swiss Alps and the date of execution: 17 September 1781. Towne's discovery of the Alps, at the age of forty, on his return from a journey to Rome (1780-1781), inspired his finest works and wrought a monumental crystallization of his style, sustained by the awe he felt at the majestic vision before him. The composition is set out vertically over a succession of crisscrossing planes delimited by incisive lines, in the manner of Oriental prints. The restricted scale of local tones vivified by the translucent light of the Swiss highlands corresponds to the various geological and spatial structures—grey and maroon for the rocks and séracs, green and blue for the mountain vegetation. The outline of the peaks is drawn in pen and ink, and the sky is full of floating clouds.

The Arveiron is a tributary of the Arve, near Mont Blanc, taking its source in a cave at the foot of the ice-covered slopes dominated by the Massif de l'Aiguille. Turner chose the same sublime site as Towne, but interpreted it differently, in the scenographic manner of Cozens. He treats it breadthwise, not as an upright; as an atmospheric fusion, not a formal abstraction; in brown modulations over a grey priming, not in overlapping tonal areas. Turner travelled through Switzerland in the summer of 1802, and this watercolour painted for his friend and patron Walter Fawkes is based on a drawing in his "St Gothard and Mont Blanc" sketchbook, the largest of his Alpine sketchbooks and the finest for the quality of the work it contains.

John Sell Cotman ▶
(1782-1842)
Chirk Aqueduct, c. 1804.
Watercolour.

John Varley
(1778-1842)
Snowdon, c. 1812-1830.
Pencil and watercolour.

As both artist and teacher John Varley was the most active of the sixteen original members of the Old Water-Colour Society founded in London in 1804. His unfinished version of *Snowdon*, the peak in North Wales familiar to most watercolourists of that day, is an astonishing achievement for its simplified forms and limpid colours. It dates from Varley's middle period, when he focused a searching eye on geometric structures and delicately recorded the interplay of warm and cool tones. The clump of trees on the right, a stock device of his, is a reminder of the historical landscapes of Claude and Poussin so much admired by the English painters. In 1802 John Sell Cotman went on a sketching tour in Wales, and from drawings made on the spot he later painted this harmoniously geometric vision of an industrial motif, the Chirk aqueduct recently built by Thomas Telford, as engineer of the Ellesmere canal. The arches rhythmically frame the patches of sky, and both are reflected back in the quiet waters.

Caspar David Friedrich
(1774-1840)
Ruins of the Abbey of Eldena
in Pomerania, c. 1820.
Pencil and watercolour.

The ruined Cistercian abbey of Eldena, near Greifswald in Pomerania, overlooking the Baltic, recurs in Friedrich's work like an obsessional motif, steeped in melancholy. The abbey ruins are often evoked in a symbolic context; sometimes, as here, with the direct realistic approach that he takes in his watercolours. The highly personal handling of colour and light pervades the objective study of the theme and transforms it into an inner vision. The German Romantics were attracted to Gothic architecture not only as a spiritual symbol, but also as a symbol of nationhood.

Karl Rottmann was commissioned in 1830 by King Ludwig I of Bavaria to paint two fresco cycles in Munich, in the arcades of the Hofgarten, one on historic Italian landscapes, the other on historic Greek landscapes. The preparatory sketches are large watercolours worked up from studies made on the spot: they are remarkable for their monumental staging and powerful grasp of Mediterranean light and colour effects.

Trained by his father, a well-known painter of ruins, Rudolf von Alt is the major watercolourist of nineteenth-century Austria and Central Europe. During his long life he kept almost exclusively to this medium, in which he tried to vie with the English and French masters. He painted chiefly landscapes, architecture and places seen during his travels in Central, Southern and Eastern Europe as far as the Crimea.

The Tivoli watercolour dates from Rudolf von Alt's first trip to Italy in 1835. It captures that unspoilt wildness of the grottoes and cascades which appealed to so many Romantic landscapists from all countries, and which Goethe described in his *Italienische Reise* under date of 16 June 1787 as "one of the great sights of nature." This early work by Alt reveals his command of an independent, spontaneous style, responsive to fluctuations of light and colour, and instinctively fitting the profusion of details into an ordered whole.

Rudolf von Alt
(1812-1905)

Gorges of the Anio
at Tivoli, 1835.
Watercolour.

Karl Rottmann
(1797-1850)

Rocky Landscape
at Pronoia near Nauplia,
Peloponnesus, 1841.
Watercolour.

Joseph Mallord William Turner
(1775-1851)
Rouen: The West Front of the Cathedral, c. 1832.
Watercolour and bodycolour with some pen on blue paper.

Richard Parkes Bonington ▶
(1802-1828)
The Leaning Towers, Bologna, c. 1826.
Watercolour.

Thanks to its natural beauties, its medieval churches, its old towns and villages, Normandy attracted many English watercolourists, among them Cotman and Bonington, and in 1820 it was the subject of the first volume of Baron Taylor's illustrated series of *Voyages pittoresques et romantiques dans l'ancienne France*. An indefatigable tourist initially trained as a topographical artist, Turner visited Normandy several times between 1821 and 1832. Following the course of the Seine and noting what he saw in his sketchbooks, Turner stopped in Rouen and systematically recorded the sights, setting and surroundings of this ancient town, dominated by its Gothic cathedral. This powerful watercolour, heightened with bodycolour on blue paper, in which architectural precision contends with the consuming power of light, numbers among the works by Turner frequently on view at the National Gallery after 1857: there Claude Monet may well have seen it during his stay in London in December 1891, just before he began painting his famous series of *Rouen Cathedral*.

Bonington toured Normandy in 1821 and two watercolours from this painting trip were exhibited with great success at the Paris Salon of 1822. In the spring of 1826 he set off for Italy with a French friend, Baron Charles Rivet, whom he had met through Delacroix and whose letters enable us to follow the course of their journey. Their destination was Venice, which they reached on the 20th of April. There they spent four weeks. Afterwards they visited Milan, Padua, Ferrara, Bologna and Florence, returning to Paris on the 20th of June.

In Venice, which had come as a revelation to Turner on his first visit there a few years before, in 1819, Bonington deepened his sense of colour by studying the old masters in the churches and museums. His views of Venice in the shifting light of the lagoon, together with this view of Bologna and its towers, show the art of Bonington at its finest, his handling at its most fluid and unerring, his chromatic sense at its most refined. His lightness of touch throws a distinctive charm over everything he painted.

John Constable
(1776-1837)
Old Sarum, 1834.
Watercolour.

This sheet, so impressionistic in its subject and the brilliance of its execution, was the first watercolour which Constable exhibited as such, in 1834, at the Royal Academy, of which he had only been made a full member in 1829, a few months after his wife's death. When, under his supervision, his engraver David Lucas made a mezzotint of it, he urged him not to lose the "solemnity" of the vision.

Almost yearly, from 1811 to 1832, Constable stayed with the Fisher family in Salisbury, where he made many pictures of the cathedral. A couple of miles to the north lie the vestiges, represented here, of the ancient town of Old Sarum, a place of national assembly under the Saxon kings. The shepherd leading his flock is the symbol of Arcadian peace and wise government as against the misuse of power and the misdeeds of war. This romantic meditation on the vicissitudes of human history unfolds in the bosom of nature, under the magnificent sweep of sky and clouds. "The sky," wrote Constable, "is the source of light in nature, and governs everything" (letter to John Fisher, 23 October 1821).

In Salisbury Plain, Wiltshire, about seven miles north of Salisbury, is Stonehenge, a circular group of huge standing stones going back to prehistoric times. This watercolour, exhibited at the Royal Academy in 1836, forms a pair with *Old Sarum*: technically it represents Constable's supreme achievement in this medium. He realized this himself, writing to his friend and future biographer C.R. Leslie on 14 September 1835: "I have made a beautiful drawing of Stone Henge; I venture to use such an expression to you." The final watercolour, preceded by two sketches made on the spot in July 1820 and three squared studies of 1835, was worked out with the care and finish of an oil painting and shows all the characteristic features of the sublime. Turner made two watercolours of Stonehenge; one, of 1828, also has a stormy sky dramatically overarching the circle of megaliths. Constable heightens the emotive power of the clouds by a double rainbow with Biblical connotations. The two human figures, one standing, the other seated, together with the hare and the wagon, are also accents of symbolic value in an imposing, awe-inspiring whole.

John Constable
(1776-1837)
Stonehenge, 1835.
Watercolour.

François Marius Granet ▶
(1775-1849)
Versailles, the Swiss Lake, c. 1840.
Pen and watercolour.

Auguste Ravier ◀
(1814-1895)
Landscape at Dusk, after 1868.
Watercolour and gouache.

Eugène Delacroix
(1798-1863)
Country Scene in England, c. 1825.
Watercolour.

During his visit to England in the summer of 1825, Delacroix loosened up his watercolour technique as a result of contacts with the Fielding brothers and Bonington. This landscape vouches for the new ease, lightness and transparency of his work. The influence of Bonington and the English watercolourists also appears in Granet, whose gravity of mood and certain compositional devices—the bare trees, the figures in back view—have a curious kinship with Caspar David Friedrich. Appointed curator of paintings at Versailles in 1826, Granet lived in a house in the park, whose gardens and ornamental basins, together with the reveries they inspired, he recorded in many watercolours.

Auguste Ravier belonged to the active and interesting regional School of Lyons, whose mystical ardour and discreet lyricism he exemplifies. After two trips to Italy in early days, where he came under the influence of Corot, Ravier settled in his native region, first at Crémieu, then at Morestel, two picturesque old towns to the east of Lyons, in the lowlands of Dauphiné, where he methodically developed his powers as a colourist. His small oils, with their impasto of pure colours over a dark underpainting, and his watercolours, some as visionary as those of Turner, record to memorable effect the mysterious glow of evening light on quiet pools of water.

William Blake
(1757-1827)
The Genius of Shakespeare, 1809.
Watercolour.

Literature and the East 6

Romanticism drew its strength from two sources: nature and the imagination. The latter force appears at its strangest in two artists in England who, turning away from landscape, painted their inner visions in figure compositions inspired by literature and mythology. One was Henry Fuseli, a Swiss of cosmopolitan background and schooling, who settled in London in 1778 after many years in Italy engrossed in the study of Michelangelo and the Mannerists. His drawings, heightened with wash and sometimes watercolour, take their themes from the same sources as his paintings, Homer, Milton, Shakespeare, the Nibelungenlied, and reveal his restless, pessimistic staginess, his love of the fantastic, his obsession with women. William Blake, who in his early work owed much to Fuseli, achieved in himself the union of painter and poet, gifted as both with lyrical, epic and prophetic genius. His creative approach was that of the medieval craftsman drawing on the divine and symbolic powers of the imagination. Blake's style was monumental even in small formats, in engraving, tempera and watercolour. He renewed the art of illustration by illuminating his own poems and those of his spiritual intercessors, Job, Milton, Dante, Shakespeare. Even while reversing its principles of linear purity and diaphanous light, he made a decisive contribution to the development of watercolour, joining up, at the opposite pole, with Turner.

The Orientalism that coincided with colonial expansion was one of the avenues of Romantic escapism. Several events helped to make it popular: Bonaparte's expedition to Egypt, accompanied by scholars and artists (1798); the Greek war of independence against the Turks, with its literary and political repercussions (1821-1830); and the French conquest of Algeria, from 1830 on, opening up North Africa to Europe.

Orientalism meant chiefly the Islamic countries around the Mediterranean basin, and a powerful literary current running from Chateaubriand and Byron to Gautier and Flaubert accompanied its artistic manifestations, whose attractions and dangers were discerned by Fromentin, himself both a writer and a painter: "The question is, whether the East lends itself to interpretation, just how far it allows of it, and whether this effort of interpretation does not mean its destruction." The East of seraglios and desert combats often provided a pretext for Western fantasies, but alongside some clever popularizers who capitalized on the vogue and ambiguity of Oriental themes there were some fine painters who tried to see the East as it really was and whose technique and vision were modified by their contacts with it.

Gros, Géricault and Bonington imagined the East without going there and created some prototypes on the strength of accessories brought back by the collector and amateur painter Vivant Denon and the painter J.R. Auguste, who did some fine watercolours. The East was by definition colourful, and watercolour was the apt medium for recording it. Like the epic East of Gros, the sensual East of Ingres—and these were the two poles of the genre—was purely imaginary. Ingres simply transformed his female bathers into odalisques by putting a turban round their heads, placing them in an exotic setting, and emphasizing the sensuous curves of his arabesques. The central theme of his work, culminating in the *Turkish Bath* (1863), is a hymn to the female body and its Oriental languors.

The first painter of the Romantic period to acquaint himself with the East at first hand and attract attention with his pictures inspired by Constantinople and Smyrna was Decamps. He was followed by Marilhat, who painted chiefly Egyptian scenes. Delacroix responded at once to the fascinations of Morocco, and his journey there in 1832 supplanted for him the journey to Italy (which he never made) by delivering him from exoticism and impelling him towards classicism. In the Moslem world of North Africa he found the noble figures of antiquity and the grandeur of Biblical landscapes which both entered later into his mural paintings. From his six months in Morocco Delacroix brought back a fabulous stock of day-to-day notes, sketches and watercolours, on which he drew, for colour and atmosphere, in all his later work. "Observe," wrote Baudelaire, "that the general colouring of Delacroix's pictures partakes of the colouring peculiar to Oriental landscapes and interiors."

Among the painters attracted to North Africa by his example, the best are Fromentin, a subtle recorder of the desert in both his paintings and his stories, and Dehodencq, a powerful colourist who worked in Andalusia before going on to Morocco. For Chassériau, it was his long stays at Constantine and Algiers which enabled him, in Théophile Gautier's words, to achieve "that exotic beauty which was his ideal, and for which he had so deep a feeling." Another French painter, Dauzats, travelled in both Egypt and Algeria, depicting what he saw with the precision of an archaeologist. Among the illustrators who travelled in the East, one of them, Constantin Guys, was a virtuoso of the watercolour. The great heirs of Delacroix's Orientalism were Renoir and Matisse, who both visited North Africa and came under the spell of its colours. England organized long-distance touring in the Levant and established its protectorate and trading stations around the isthmus of Suez. Among its intrepid travellers and Orientalists were such proficient watercolourists as David Roberts, W.J. Müller, Edward Lear and W.H. Hunt. The most famous of them was John Frederick Lewis, who lived for ten years in Cairo, where he adopted the customs of the country and received a visit from Thackeray in 1844. On his return to London in 1851, Lewis created a sensation with his brightly coloured, carefully finished watercolours of Egyptian harems.

Charles Gleyre, in Switzerland, obtained a similar success with Eastern themes. The outstanding Orientalists in Austria were Leopold Karl Müller and Ludwig Deutsch, and in Italy Alberto Pasini. The foremost Orientalists of the Symbolist generation in France were Gustave Moreau and Paul Gauguin, but for both of them the term must be taken in its widest meaning. Moreau was intent on the literary myths of ancient culture, Gauguin on the barbarian myths of primitive life.

Henry Fuseli
(1741-1825)
Nightmare Leaving the Bed
of Two Sleeping Women, 1810.
Pencil and watercolour.

This light-toned, almost monochrome watercolour is dated on the lower right: 28 May-4 June 1810. On the lower left it bears an inscription in Greek, in Fuseli's hand, from the *Iliad* (X, 496-497), reading: "Rhesus breathed hard, for like to an evil dream there stood above his head that night the son of Oeneus' son, by the device of Athene." There is an earlier oil painting, of about 1793, with the same composition (Muraltengut, Zurich), but Fuseli's initial painting on the Nightmare theme, done in several versions,

goes back to 1781 (Detroit Institute of Arts and Goethe-Museum, Frankfurt). It represents a single female sleeper, lying on her back with an incubus seated on her breast, while the horrified head of a horse looks in through the curtains. Associated with the sun, the horse is also the embodiment of desire and the symbol of nocturnal phantasms. A contemporary of Sade and Goya, Fuseli too depicted the dark spectres of demonism and delivered up his idol Woman to the forces of terror and destruction.

In the autumn of 1824, encouraged by his young admirers and disciples John Linnell and Samuel Palmer, Blake undertook a series of watercolour illustrations for the *Divine Comedy*, unfinished at his death in August 1827. At sixty-seven he began studying Italian, to read the text in the original language. Dante was one of his spiritual heroes and a fellow recorder of "visions of eternity," but Blake did not share his theological views, Christianity being for Blake the religion of forgiveness, not punishment. His Dante illustrations were not a mere accompaniment but a reinterpretation. Of the 102 watercolours which he completed, he only had time to engrave seven. This one, sublime in its imaginative power, illustrates Canto XXIX of the Purgatorio, with Beatrice appearing to Dante on her chariot drawn by a griffin. The rainbow colours shimmer like precious stones in the supernatural light, and each colour has its metaphorical value, red standing for feeling and blue for wisdom or imagination.

William Blake
(1757-1827)
Beatrice Addressing Dante
from the Car, 1824-1827.
Watercolour.

According to his pupil Montfort, who made his career as an Orientalist, and his biographer Clément, Géricault met by chance, in the streets of Paris, a group of shipwrecked Turks and hired one of them, Mustapha, as his servant. This simple, monumental portrait of him, probably painted after Géricault's visit to London in 1820-1821, speaks for his mastery of the watercolour technique and his human insight and empathy. The nostalgic face of this Turk stranded in Paris served as a model for many of the Oriental subjects treated by Géricault.

Thanks to their nimble mounts, Arab horsemen are able to execute at a gallop the boldest turns and moves, while firing in the air and uttering war cries. During his journey to Morocco, Delacroix witnessed these equestrian displays, known as fantasias, on arriving at Meknes on 15 March 1832. He wrote to his friend Pierret: "Our entry here was extremely fine, such a pleasure as one can hope to experience but once in a lifetime... At every moment we were met with new tribes, armed and mounted, who expended a terrific amount of gunpowder to celebrate our arrival."

Théodore Géricault
(1791-1824)
Bedouin with his Horse.
Pencil and watercolour.

Eugène Delacroix
(1798-1863)
Fantasia at the Gate
of Meknes, 1832.
Watercolour.

Eugène Delacroix
(1798-1863)
Moorish Conversation, 1832.
Watercolour.

Delacroix landed at Toulon on 5 July 1832 after a journey of six months through Morocco. During the forced leisure of quarantine in the lazaretto of Toulon harbour, he worked on an album of eighteen watercolours recording his impressions of North Africa and presented it to Count Charles de Mornay, who had led the French mission to Morocco and was also a well-known collector. This fine sheet comes from the Mornay album which, after the Count's death, was broken up and sold by auction at the Hôtel Drouot, Paris, on 29 March 1877.

Fromentin commented on Delacroix's Oriental scenes: "He saw these men dressed, and consequently their shape, their gestures and a vague sight of their face, but he caught the costume and colour splendidly... Of the East he recorded the strong blues of its sky, its livid shadows, its soft half-tones... He had no scruple about substituting a green countryside for its burnt-out horizons: he took the landscape as a prop, a deep and muted accompaniment which set off, sustained and enhanced a hundredfold the magnificent sonorities of his colouring."

Ingres set store by line, but as he said "there is no example of a great draughtsman who failed to find the colouring exactly suited to the character of his drawings." At eighty-four he still drew deftly, firmly, unerringly, the heady arabesques of the female body, which he described as "straight planes with full curves," and then laid in his local tones in flat areas, with the freshness and brightness of Persian miniatures. This watercolour dated 1864, his eighty-fourth year, is the end-point of a long series on the obsessional theme that runs through his entire work: the seated bather in back view, with crossed legs and stylized elongations, transformed by the turban into an odalisque. Here she stands out against an Oriental setting in which reappear various figures of the *Turkish Bath*, finished the year before: the Negress with a tambourine, the dancing slave girl, and the languid courtisans.

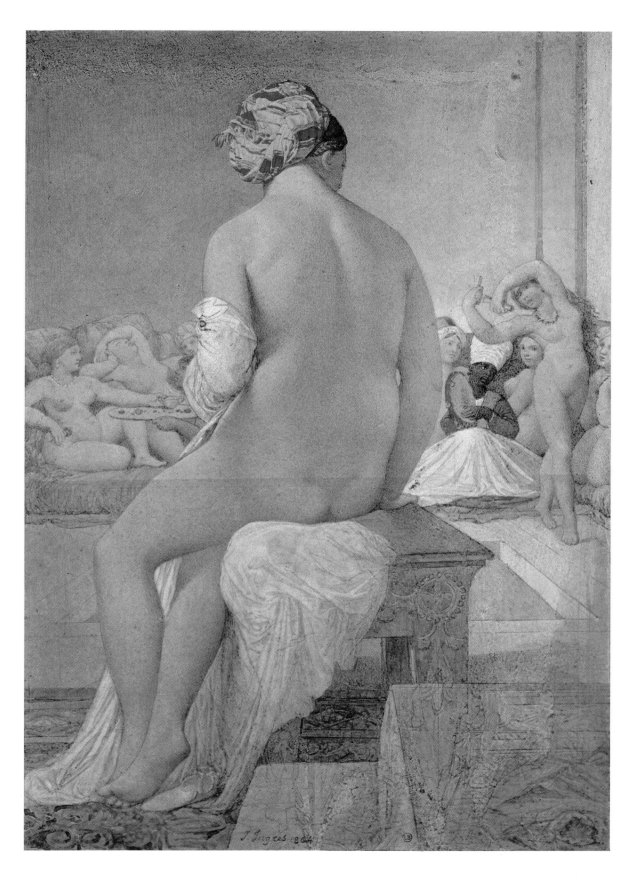

Jean-Auguste-Dominique Ingres
(1780-1867)
Odalisque, 1864.
Watercolour.

Théodore Chassériau
(1819-1856)
Negress of Algiers, 1846.
Pencil and watercolour.

"A graphic chronicler of the splendours and miseries of modern woman" (as Henri Focillon called him), Constantin Guys depicted her as he saw her in different countries and social classes. Already a seasoned traveller, he was sent out to the Crimea as war artist for the *Illustrated London News*, and in Constantinople in 1856 he drew not only the official ceremonies and feast-days but also the picturesque low life of the streets. This prostitute in the Galata quarter was probably of foreign birth and wears a national costume thus described by Baudelaire in his famous essay on Guys: "the embroidered, short-sleeved jackets, the falling sash, the ample pantaloons, the upturned Turkish slippers, the striped or spangled muslins, and all the finery of her native land." Over an initial pencil sketch reworked with pen and ink, the light colours were applied in shimmering washes.

◄ **Constantin Guys**
(1802-1892)
Turkish Prostitute at Galata, Constantinople, 1856.
Pencil, pen and watercolour.

Early in 1845, while on a visit to Paris, the Caliph of Constantine in Algeria commissioned Chassériau to paint his portrait, made friends with the young painter during the sittings, and invited him to stay with him in his North African palace. On arriving there in the spring of 1846, Chassériau wrote to his brother: "The country is very fine and wholly new to me. I live here as they do in the Thousand and One Nights. I think I'll be able to turn it to advantage in my art." Like Delacroix, whose example stimulated him, he made watercolour sketches of the sights and scenes around him. His aim as he noted in his travel diary, was to record "these rugged, colourful figures in bright Oriental colours against a white ground." The *Negress* is one of these figure studies, made in Algiers as Chassériau was about to sail for France after his stay in Constantine. On it he wrote: "Negress with lilac tones, the robe with Cashmere designs."

The sheet by John Frederick Lewis is one of his many harem pictures, painted from firsthand knowledge of Cairo life. They were highly successful when exhibited in London at the Old Water-Colour Society, of which Lewis was elected president in 1855. Ruskin, in a pamphlet on the Society's 1856 exhibition, dilated on the finish and refinements of Lewis's pictures, calling on his readers to examine them with a magnifying glass. Their wealth of decorative detail is rendered with the same geometric accuracy as in Vermeer's interiors and those of the Dutch little masters.

John Frederick Lewis
(1805-1876)
Life in the Harem, Cairo, 1841-1851.
Watercolour.

Gustave Moreau
(1826-1898)

Phaethon, before 1878.
Black chalk and watercolour
heightened with white and varnish.

Paul Gauguin
(1848-1903)
Tahitian Landscape, 1891-1893.
Watercolour.

After visiting the Paris World's Fair of 1878 where Gustave Moreau's large watercolour *Phaethon* was prominently exhibited, Odilon Redon wrote in his diary (published as *A soi-même*, Paris, 1922): "In the vividness of these nuances, in the bold divergence of the lines, in the mordant harshness of these bright colours, there is grandeur and emotion, and something of a new wonder." At the fatal moment when Phaethon loses control of the chariot of the sun, its fall sets off a great burst of sunlight, and the rash boy haloed with golden rays, with the monstrous Python rearing up from the underworld, shrinks back from the lion, the symbol of solar energy, leaping down at him with a roar from the vault of heaven.

Nothing could better evoke the island beauty of Oceania than this magnificent watercolour painted by Gauguin in his early days in Tahiti and pasted on page 179 of the manuscript of *Noa Noa*, a diary of his mental life and preoccupations on the "fragrant" island. In it Gauguin wrote: "Wishing to suggest a lush, overgrown nature and a tropical sun blazing over it all, I had to give my figures a corresponding setting... Hence all these fabulous colours and this blazing but subdued and silent atmosphere." This same landscape, transposed into the iridescent pink and violet of his final period, serves as the background of one of Gauguin's last paintings, done in March 1903: *Three Women and White Horse* (Museum of Fine Arts, Boston).

Honoré Daumier
(1808-1879)

The Connoisseur.
Watercolour and gouache
over black chalk.

From Realism to Impressionism

7

Realism, in reaction against romanticism, rejected the exotic and picturesque. To both daily life and the social sphere it applied that accuracy of observation which had been introduced into landscape, now the dominant branch of painting. The two leading painters of the Barbizon School, for whom the cult of nature was the new religion, were Jean-François Millet and Théodore Rousseau: they painted only a few watercolours, of an intense sobriety. The realist current centred on the human figure instead of nature, and the figure in its urban setting, derived from the caricature of manners. The modern caricature, whose artistic value and historical significance were recognized by Baudelaire, and which Goya carried to its highest pitch in his prints, originated in England with Thomas Rowlandson, James Gillray and George Cruikshank: all three expressed themselves in watercolours and coloured prints. Then caricature was taken up in France, where it was stimulated by the growth of the press and the spread of a graphic medium as quick and spirited as drawing: lithography. There watercolour and lithography went hand in hand, answering to the same need for promptness and spontaneity. Such French caricaturists and illustrators as Nicolas-Toussaint Charlet, Henry Monnier, Gavarni and Gustave Doré, all of them anglophiles moreover, practised watercolour and lithography simultaneously with unfailing verve, but Daumier outdid them all by the power and range of his genius. Of Daumier it has been said, and rightly said, that his graphic output matches the literary output of Balzac, and that he achieves in the comic vein a universality comparable to that of Molière, his favourite author. His lithographs represent the public side of his work. For its private side we have to go to his watercolours, with their highly personal handling in which the tonality of the wash fits so perfectly into the structure of the design, and their ever varying treatment of a few essential themes—art lovers, the theatre, the railway carriage.

Courbet, the head of the realist school, was, like Caravaggio or Frans Hals, so fully in possession of his craft that he rarely did any drawing and his tonal painting is opposed to the bright clear hues of watercolour. Corot drew a great deal, but watercolour was not his medium either; he made only a few private experiments in it towards the end of his life. Several landscapists marked by Corot's example were regular and delicate watercolourists: Chintreuil, who worked in the Mantes region, and Harpignies, who worked around Rome and later all over France. The pre-Impressionists Boudin and Jongkind, who painted together on the coast of Normandy, where they were coached by Isabey, a powerful watercolourist, both proved bolder and freer in their watercolours than in their oils. Called by Corot "the monarch of the skies," and ever responsive, as Baudelaire noted, to "meteorological beauties," Boudin worked chiefly in his native Normandy, painting the beaches of Deauville and Trouville, where the figures of fashionably dressed ladies stand out in vivid tones against the shifting luminosity of sea and sky. Boudin's exquisite pictures, even with their faintly English imprint, are like a delightful echo of Guardi. With Jongkind, wrote the critic Castagnary in 1863, "everything lies in the impression." This clear-eyed, sure-handed Dutchman, active chiefly in France, had an innate sense of space and light. His forthright watercolours, washed in over a concise, unerring design, were admirably analyzed by Paul Signac, who gave them their rightful place between Turner and Cézanne. The brilliant chroniclers of their time, Constantin Guys and Eugène Lami, were both virtuosos of watercolour painting.

The culmination and distillation of realism, with no social implications and no emotional charge, Impressionism rests on the purity of optical sensations and the magic of visual appearances. The vibrancy of light breaks down contours and dissolves the motif into colour patches flickering in the radiance of the atmosphere. Monet and Sisley painted no watercolours, for they generalized the open style of the sketch, handling oil paints in the manner of watercolours, even setting them off with unpainted areas of the canvas. Manet and Degas, who both received the classical training, finished off in watercolour the preparatory drawings for their early figure compositions, but later preferred pastel. Renoir experimented successfully with all the colour techniques, in particular red chalk and watercolour. Berthe Morisot, gravitating around Manet, then Renoir, asserted her feminine grace and her own peculiar gifts. As an interpreter of childhood and motherhood in their domestic setting, she turned naturally to watercolour, which she applied in deft touches, "as if," wrote Théodore Duret, "she were plucking off the petals of flowers." Seurat, the creator of Divisionism or Pointillism, drew with the Conté crayon and used oil paints directly for his preparatory sketches on small wooden panels. With Pissarro, watercolour came to the fore only during his Pointillist phase, and the same is true of his friend Van Gogh, who during his stay in Paris (1886-1888) was chiefly in touch with the group around Seurat. The latter's best disciples, Signac and Cross, painted many watercolours after 1900, with a new expressiveness and bolder tones that point the way to Fauvism.

Of the great American painters contemporary with Impressionism, two remained at home and carried on the national tradition, Eakins and Homer, while three worked in Europe, Mary Cassatt, Whistler and Sargent. Akin to Degas, Mary Cassatt produced a large body of pastels and colour prints. Whistler was friendly with Courbet, and Sargent with Monet: both were aesthetes and men of the world, at ease in the fashionable society of London and Paris, and in their later years both Whistler and Sargent painted some masterly landscape watercolours, steeped in their personal sensibility, which form a happy contrast with their lifelong activity as portraitists. Eakins, in Philadelphia, was a realist painter intent on scientific accuracy, and when he turned to watercolours he adopted the unusual procedure of making preparatory studies for them in oils. Eakins was a close friend of Walt Whitman, but the true counterpart in painting of the great American poet was Winslow Homer, a New Englander, whose fine watercolours express with commanding power his physical communion with nature and elemental life.

Honoré Daumier
(1808-1879)
Showmen at a Fair Booth, 1867-1870.
Crayon and watercolour,
with traces of red chalk.

The theatre in all its aspects, both actors and audience, was a favourite theme with Daumier. The theatre as such is evoked chiefly in his paintings and lithographs, the side-show and street performers in his watercolours and drawings. Like his friend Baudelaire, Daumier felt the underlying kinship between the artist and the showman, both outsiders in modern society—a theme taken up later by Picasso, Rouault, Rilke and Apollinaire. One of his finest pictures of showmen is the Louvre watercolour, with traces of red chalk, datable to 1867-1870, for which he made several preliminary drawings. It represents *la parade*, the outside show or knockabout turn given by the travelling players, to attract the public, before the performance inside the booth. The mountebank leans on the railing with both arms, doing his best to stir up the crowd, and the barker beside him keeps up a running flow of patter, pointing with his wand to the backdrop, where a crocodile with gaping jaws pursues a fleeing figure.

The railway compartment is like an itinerant theatre where the human comedy is played out in silence in a closed space. The famous set of Daumier watercolours in Baltimore representing the first, second and third class carriages are like a cross-section of nineteenth-century French society. They are at once historical documents and artistic masterpieces. They were commissioned directly from the artist by George A. Lucas, a retired American railway engineer then living in Paris; and for two of them, including this one, the exact date of the order, 28 April 1864, is recorded in Lucas's diary (preserved in the Peabody Institute, Baltimore). Avoiding anecdote, Daumier concentrated on the faces of the four half-length figures sitting in a row, lit up obliquely by light from the windows (one unseen). Brought together by chance, they ignore each other and keep silent. The two men are absorbed in their thoughts; one woman gazes out of the carriage window, the other is reading.

Honoré Daumier
(1808-1879)
The First Class Compartment, 1864.
Pencil, watercolour and gouache.

Most of Berthe Morisot's watercolours represent the women around her at home, her sisters, her daughter Julie, her female cousins and friends. This one, dating to the early 1870s, is a preparatory study for one of her paintings: it shows her younger sister Edma Pontillon and her niece Paule Gobillard on the balcony of their apartment overlooking Paris, with the dome of the Invalides visible on the right. "It is made out of nothing," wrote Paul Valéry (who married Paule's sister Nini Gobillard), "but this skimming touch conveys everything: the time, place and season. Such were her skill and promptitude, her great gift of going to essentials, of lightening the paints to the extreme and thereby carrying to its highest point the impression of an act of the mind."

Berthe Morisot
(1841-1895)
On the Balcony, 1872.
Pencil and watercolour.

A man of the lower middle class, close to the people, Boudin admitted to feeling ill at ease in the presence of the "idle rich" at the fashionable seaside resorts on the Channel coast, in Normandy; but, he added, justifying himself, "since landscape has its painters of predilection, do not these bourgeois strolling on the pier have the right to be fixed on canvas too and set in the light?" For light absorbs and purifies everything, removes the social implications of the subject and transforms it into an artistic motif. Here the setting and elegant figures were sketched out in pencil, then built up in transparent washes of ash-grey and pink.

In the summer of 1880, to beguile the solitude of his course of treatment at Bellevue, just outside Paris, Manet wrote some short letters, witty or tender, usually illustrated, to his lady friends and in particular to Isabelle Lemonnier, daughter of a well-known Paris jeweller, then on holiday at Loc-sur-Mer. This graceful watercolour, added to one of his letters, and done from memory or a photograph, shows her on a summer outing with her black sunshade held under her arm.

Edouard Manet
(1832-1883)
Isabelle Lemonnier, 1880.
Watercolour.

Eugène Boudin
(1824-1898)
Figures on a Beach in Normandy.
Pencil and watercolour.

During his academic training at The Hague in the 1830s, Jongkind learned the watercolour technique from his master Schelfhout, but it was only after 1860 that watercolours, on which he noted the date and place of execution, began to bulk large in his work, and they answer best to the spontaneity of his genius. From 1861 to 1865 Jongkind spent the summer months on the coast of Normandy, where he saw much of Boudin, Daubigny and Monet. In the summer of 1866, on the way home to Holland, he stopped at Antwerp: there, from early September to mid-October, he painted the shipping from the banks of the Scheldt in a series of about forty watercolours. This one, dated the 15th of September, is one of the finest in his whole output. Silhouetted on the horizon is the tower of the village of Oosterweel, serving as a landmark under the broad sky and indicating the point on the estuary from which the painter was working. Of Jongkind, Paul Signac wrote admiringly: "From 1863 on, working from motifs at Honfleur, Antwerp, Rotterdam and the environs of Paris, he painted the finest series of watercolours in the world. In them his pencil attains its highest pitch of expression, his colour its fullest harmony and significance."

Johan Barthold Jongkind
(1819-1891)

View over the Scheldt at Antwerp, 1866.
Watercolour.

Like his compatriot Jongkind, Vincent van Gogh loved the sweep of light over vast spaces. He practised watercolour painting from his early Dutch period, and during his stay in Paris (1886-1888) he succeeded in combining the wealth of colour acquired from Impressionism with the strength of line inherent in his own temperament. In the spring and summer of 1887 he often went on painting trips outside Paris, towards Asnières or Saint-Ouen, with Emile Bernard and Paul Signac. It was then that he took up Pointillism and, acting on the example of Seurat and Luce, drew or painted views of the industrial suburbs, with factories and workmen's housing. The blank space left in the foreground, linking up rhythmically with the curving road and the distant strip of sky, is a compositional device often used by Van Gogh.

Vincent van Gogh
(1853-1890)
Industrial Suburb, Paris, 1887.
Watercolour.

Camille Pissarro
(1830-1903)
Funeral of Cardinal de Bonnechose
at Rouen, 1883.
Pencil and watercolour.

Paul Signac ◄
(1863-1935)
The Port of Saint-Tropez, 1901.
Pencil and watercolour.

Henri-Edmond Cross ►
(1856-1910)
Trees by the Sea, c. 1906-1907.
Pencil and watercolour.

Pissarro left a large body of graphic work, covering a variety of themes and media. Watercolour he used most often in the intermediate phase, in the 1880s, between Impressionism and Pointillism, to which he was attracted for several years. In the autumn of 1883 he made his first long stay at Rouen, to which he was to return several times, and there in November he witnessed the great public funeral, on the Place de la République, of Cardinal de Bonnechose, who had been Archbishop of Rouen since 1858. This crowd scene, all in light and vivid touches of colour, is like a foretaste of the overhead views of crowded Paris streets which Pissarro painted repeatedly after 1897.

Paul Signac, who acted as the link between Seurat and Pissarro, was an outstanding practitioner and theorist of watercolour painting. His annotated watercolour sketchbooks contain some unknown masterpieces. A keen sailor and yachtsman, he painted many harbour scenes, from Rotterdam to Constantinople. In 1892, on one of his cruises, Signac discovered Saint-Tropez on the French Riviera, then a solitary fishing village accessible only by sea, and there built his villa La Hune. His friend Cross lived near by at Saint-Clair. Often working together on the Riviera in the early 1900s, they captured the glowing Mediterranean light in some bold watercolours and prepared the way for Fauvism.

James McNeill Whistler
(1834-1903)
Southend Pier, Essex, c. 1884.
Watercolour.

Whistler is famous for his large portraits and his decorative paintings of Japanese inspiration, but the most appealing and still little known side of his work is to be found in his oil sketches on panel, his Venetian etchings and pastels (both of the highest quality), his Paris lithographs with their sensitive grasp of neighbourhood life, and the radiant watercolours of his middle period, mostly beach and river scenes in England and Holland. These last, signed with the famous butterfly monogram, figured in his one-man show of 1884 at the Dowdeswell Gallery, London, which also included the recent watercolours done at St Ives in Cornwall. Though close to the Impressionists in many ways, Whistler kept to tonal values and refined, highly personal harmonies of grey and silver. His allusive grace and subjective poetry links him with the Symbolist movement and won him the admiration of Mallarmé, Debussy and Proust.

Whistler and Homer represent two radically opposed temperaments: the cosmopolitan aesthete steeped in urban culture, and the retiring lover of rural life and unspoilt nature. Homer's watercolours of the period 1873-1905 stand out as the finest, most original achievement of this great New England realist, whose two visits to Europe (France, 1866-1867, and England, 1881-1883) made no change in his naive, independent vision. He was conscious of their importance and declared that he would be remembered for his watercolours. They fall into two main series: those inspired by his hunting and fishing trips in the Adirondacks and Canada, and the late ones evoking the tropical splendour of the Bahamas (and contemporary with Gauguin's work in Tahiti and the Marquesas). Homer's watercolours directly record not the painter's feelings but his physical sensations and the vitality of the elements, with fluid touches of colour of exceptional freshness.

Winslow Homer
(1836-1910)
The Adirondack Guide, 1894.
Watercolour.

Paul Cézanne
(1839-1906)
Young Man with a Red Waistcoat, 1889-1890.
Watercolour.

Cézanne and His Legacy

8

The art of Cézanne is a complex realization of two things: the sensations aroused in him by nature, truthfully recorded, and the internal exigencies of the plane surface on which form and colour had to be made to coexist. "When colour is at its richest," he said, "form is at its fullest." Though many of his watercolours were destroyed or lost, over six hundred of them remain. They follow a line of development parallel to his oil paintings, but independent of it, reflecting the successive stages of his growth as an artist, through his romantic, impressionist and constructive periods; and during his final period, when they became preponderant, their lyricism reacted on his painting and they then acquired their full autonomy and power of radiance. The painter Emile Bernard was able to watch Cézanne at work on a watercolour, on the slopes of Les Lauves at Aix, in 1904: "He began on the shadow with a single patch of colour, which he then overlapped with a second, then a third, until all these tints, forming successive screens, not only coloured the object but modelled its form." These coats of superimposed, transparent colours, which went to create the shadows, were unified by the white, light-generating surface of the paper, which plays so essential a part in watercolour paintings. Sometimes a few fluctuating lines of blue were laid in with the brush to readjust forms and integrate them into the wave-flow of light. Already shown separately by Vollard in the summer of 1905, Cézanne's late watercolours were exhibited again in Paris at the Bernheim-Jeune Gallery, in June 1907, a few months before the historic Cézanne retrospective at the Salon d'Automne, devoted chiefly to the oil paintings. These watercolours aroused the admiration of the younger painters, and Rainer Maria Rilke, who saw the exhibition, described them as being "like the echo of a melody." Their influence was felt increasingly on all aspects of contemporary art, most intensely during the revolutionary years 1907-1914, when they were exhibited by turn in Berlin, New York, Cologne, London, Brussels, Rome and Dresden.

Before forging their new art language, the two pioneers of Cubism, Braque and Picasso, referred back to Cézanne, whom they took as their spiritual guide and artistic mediator. And the initial phase of their venture, the geometric restructuring of form, is rightly known as the Cézannian phase. The opening out of volumes and their internal fragmentation by the system of patterned facets, that is the homogeneous reorganization of form on the level of the plane surface, characterized the analytical phase of Cubism, pressed to the limits of abstraction. The final step in that direction was taken by Kandinsky and Delaunay who, each in his own way, continued Cézanne's experiments with colour, which had been provisionally abandoned by Cubism in its initial concentration on the problem of space. It was through the experimental medium of watercolour, at the very time when he was writing his profession of faith, *Concerning the Spiritual in Art*, that Kandinsky, as if in a burst of mystical wonder, painted his first abstract watercolour (1910). Delaunay, who expressed his admiration for Cézanne's watercolours, departed from Cubism and made his way to abstraction through the "orphic" power of colour, which with him is at once form, subject and movement. His innovations, transmitted also by his writings, were developed in their own terms by his friends Chagall and Léger, by the Blaue Reiter in Germany, and by the Rayonists in Russia. With Futurism, whose main representative as both painter and sculptor was Boccioni, there came a lively and polemical working out of the notion of simultaneity, in which Léger too was involved. "Cézanne," acknowledged Léger, "taught me the love of forms and volumes. He led me to concentrate on drawing." After fighting what he called "the battle of volumes" by reducing the role of colour, Léger went on to base his pictorial dynamics on "the intensity of contrasts" between the saturation of the three primary colours and the purity of geometric forms. Preferring gouache to watercolour, he used the latter only during a short and luminous period.

A friend of Kandinsky from 1911, Klee paid a visit to Delaunay in Paris in the autumn of 1912, when the latter's colours were at their most radiant, and translated into German Delaunay's essay *Sur la lumière*. In the spring of 1914, accompanied by Louis Moilliet and August Macke, Klee made a journey to Tunisia. For him, as for Delacroix, North Africa was a decisive revelation, which he recorded in a series of watercolours. Drinking in the light and atmosphere of Kairouan, in the interior, he noted in his diary (16 April 1914): "It's all pouring into me so deeply and gently, I can feel it and am gaining confidence, without any effort. Colour has taken hold of me... That is the meaning of this happy hour: colour and I are one. I'm a painter." From then on, growing on the firm basis of his innate sense of line and design, Klee's work is like an unbroken piece of chamber music with ever varied harmonies. Working on a variety of surfaces in many different media, including watercolour, Klee devised an alchemy all his own from which he distilled, in small but inimitable pictures, his poetics of colour.

From 1922 on, Klee and Kandinsky were fellow teachers at the Bauhaus, where they worked in fruitful emulation. The Bauhaus engraving workshop was directed by an American artist, Lyonel Feininger, who had lived in Germany since 1887: among his finest works are his watercolour seascapes with their delicate network of lines and their subdued lighting. Another Bauhaus master was Oskar Schlemmer, in charge of the stage design workshop. He developed a multiform, mechanistic treatment of the human figure in its various postures. Towards the end of his life, in the 1930s, he turned to watercolour, a medium more in keeping with the growing freedom and flexibility of his style.

After Winslow Homer, the great American master of watercolour was John Marin. His earliest ones go back to about 1887, and in fact he did not take up oil painting till after 1925, and his watercolours remain his finest work. He lived in Europe, mostly in Paris, from 1905 to 1911, and assimilated into his personal style the new trends from Cézanne to Delaunay. After returning to New York in 1912, Marin successfully recorded in fluid colours and energetic brushstrokes the restless movement of American city life and the atmospheric light playing over its architecture.

Paul Cézanne
(1839-1906)
Landscape in Provence, c. 1880.
Watercolour.

Cézanne's watercolours, like his oil paintings, consist of landscapes, portraits, still lifes and figure compositions. Landscape dominated during his constructive period when he painted this fine *Landscape in Provence*. The linear underpinnings give way to an upsurge of colour-forms and their light vibrations. Two clumps of trees with exuberant leafage, a darker one on the left, a brighter one on the right, frame the central zone occupied successively by the sheet of water, the volumetric house, sunny patches of soil and the mountain closing off the horizon. The colour scheme is a combination of blues and greens of all shades, set off by a few accents of ochre and red.

In the later *Still Life with Apples, Pears and Saucepan*, the rounded shapes of the fruit are set out with sensual simplicity on the kitchen table. Here the three primary colours, red, yellow and blue, are ordered with masterly ease and luminous fluidity. The point of convergence is marked by the violet-blue handle of the saucepan, with its forceful outward thrust.

The Mont Sainte-Victoire with its translucent cone dominates the Aix countryside like a symbol of Provence. In the later years of his life it became Cézanne's most frequent, most characteristic theme, as he recorded it, near or far, from various familiar spots. In November 1901 he purchased a piece of ground on the upward slope of Les Lauves, where he built himself a studio. From then until his death in 1906 Cézanne painted a series of about twenty watercolours, showing the majestic view from the crest of Les Lauves over the Sainte-Victoire mountain and the surrounding plain. The one reproduced here, in Dublin, is perhaps the least known and yet one of the finest and most aerial, with its gossamer light touches of green, blue and pink, musically orchestrating space and letting the white of the paper shine through.

Paul Cézanne
(1839-1906)
Mont Sainte-Victoire Seen from
Les Lauves, 1901-1906.
Pencil and watercolour.

Paul Cézanne
(1839-1906)

Still Life with Apples, Pears
and Saucepan, 1900-1904.
Pencil and watercolour.

In July 1907 Picasso finished, or stopped work on, the *Demoiselles d'Avignon*, the volcanic painting that overthrew naturalistic conventions and shifted the centre of gravity to the creative act and its clashing tensions. There followed, on the same expressionist and "barbaric" lines but in more distinctly Cézannian terms, two further figure compositions: *Friendship*, representing two women, painted in the winter, and *Three Women*, painted in the spring of 1908. Both are now in the Hermitage Museum, Leningrad, and both were prepared by an extraordinary sequence of watercolours and gouaches. The powerful watercolour of *Five Women*, five nude bathers whose rhythmically flexed and bending bodies are interwoven with the trees of the forest, also dates from the spring of 1908 and combines the two previous groups. It was not worked up into an oil painting.

It was chiefly during his "mechanical" period, from 1917 to 1923, that Léger sometimes used watercolour instead of the gouache which he preferred. He did not imitate the outward form of machines and industrial objects, but transposed their general features into his cubist syntax, thereby conveying their structure and workings. "I have turned to the mechanical element," he said, "not for its own sake or mine, but as a means of conveying a sensation of force and power." Machinery for Léger was not the idol set up by the Futurists and Constructivists, nor the monster denounced by the Dadaists. It was the symbol and reality of modern society, and as such it stood at the centre of modern art. "I have never bothered to copy a machine. I invent pictures of machines as others make up landscapes out of their imagination."

A painter, sculptor and theorist, Boccioni was the dominant personality of Futurism. A Calabrian, working mostly in Rome and Milan, he made several stays in Paris where he had some friendly but polemical give-and-take with both Léger and Delaunay. Boccioni's art is based on the interpenetration of coloured planes and dynamic lines of force. His last works, drawings, watercolours and gouaches, done just before he was killed by a fall from his horse in 1916, while serving in the Italian army, mark a return to Cézanne.

◄Pablo Picasso
(1881-1973)
Five Women (Bathers
in a Forest), 1908.
Pencil and watercolour.

Fernand Léger ►
(1881-1955)
Composition, 1917.
Watercolour.

Umberto Boccioni
(1882-1916)
Dynamic Plastic Composition,
Horse + Rider + House, 1914.
Pencil and watercolour.

Spirited lines and patches of colour, shaped by an "inner necessity" (Kandinsky's own words) with no reference to the visible world, float organically in a dematerialized space. The date Kandinsky gave for his first abstract watercolour, 1910, has been questioned, for the equivalent oils radically breaking the link with reality do not appear in his work till 1913. There are, however, good reasons for accepting the 1910 dating, in particular the essential fact that Kandinsky's essay *Über das Geistige in der Kunst* (Concerning the Spiritual in Art), though not published till 1912, was written in 1910 and expressly announces the advent of "emancipated painting" in the form of "pure composition."

With Delaunay, there was no systematic transition to abstraction, and representational allusions continued to appear in the whirl of colours. Like Jacques Villon and Roger de La Fresnaye, he was keenly interested in the exploits of the pioneer aviators. This *Homage to Blériot* is a sketch for the large oil painting in the Basel Museum. The rhythm is created by a dynamic pattern of circular forms, through which rise the silhouette of the Eiffel Tower and the propellers of an airplane.

Like Delaunay, who repeatedly painted the Eiffel Tower in Paris, John Marin was fascinated by the buildings of lower Manhattan. He was stimulated, as the Futurists were, by the unprecedented dynamism of the modern city. "I try to express graphically what a great city is doing," he wrote. "Within the frames there must be balance, a controlling of these warring, pushing, pulling forces." From 1914 on, Marin spent the summers on the Maine coast, painting watercolour seascapes, and proved himself to be also a great marine painter.

90

John Marin
(1870-1953)
Municipal Building, New York, 1912.
Watercolour.

Louis Moilliet
(1880-1962)
Kairouan, 1914.
Watercolour.

August Macke
(1887-1914)
Kairouan I, 1914.
Watercolour.

92

1914 / 217 St.germain b Tunis (landeinwärts)

Paul Klee
(1879-1940)
Saint-Germain near Tunis
(looking inland), 1914.
Watercolour.

In the spring of 1914 the Swiss painter Louis Moilliet, trained and living in Germany, was invited to Tunisia for the second time by a Bernese doctor practising there, Dr Jäggi. Moilliet invited his friends Paul Klee and August Macke to go with him. The three young painters sailed from Marseilles and reached Tunis on the 7th of April. Klee's diary records the profusion of sensations he took in, the sights, smells and music of the place, and notes the successive stages of this short but decisive journey. After exploring Tunis, and some trips by car into the interior, they spent Easter Sunday, 11 April, at Dr Jäggi's country house at Saint-Germain, on the Gulf of Tunis, where they did a series of watercolours, some focused on the sea, some on the hinterland. "The evening is indescribable. Moreover the moon is rising." Failing to catch that moonrise in paints, Klee added: "But there is no point in being in a hurry when one requires so much of oneself. This evening has entered into me deeply, now and for always."

Then came the majestic uphill journey to Sidi-bou-Saïd and the enchanted pause in the port of Hammamet, where Klee "lived poetically," the "ever unforgettable cadence" of the tambourine mingling with the exhilarating sights and smells. Finally, on 15 April, came the revelation of Kairouan, "a place very much like me," where he felt the "Arab marriage" of mind and senses and gained his new understanding of colour. Back in Tunis on the 19th, Klee was impatient to start for home, "the wagon overloaded" with impressions, and left his two friends, who wished to stay a few days more. While Moilliet's notations remained sketchy, though delicately coloured, Macke's watercolours and those of Klee even more achieve a fine synthesis between the chromatic innovations of Cézanne and Delaunay. Macke's career was cut short by the war: he was killed in action on 26 September 1914. Moilliet gave up oil painting in 1917 and thereafter worked exclusively in watercolours.

93

Paul Klee ▶
(1879-1940)
Portal of a Mosque, 1931.
Watercolour.

◀ **Lyonel Feininger**
(1871-1956)
Harbour Entrance, 1927.
Pen and watercolour.

Paul Klee
(1879-1940)
Tree with Houses, 1918.
Watercolour.

Klee liked to vary his painting surfaces, he liked the effects to be obtained from papers of various grain or from fabrics. His *Tree with Houses* was done on a strip of gauze, whose visible mesh absorbs the paints and modifies their nature and radiance. Over this full-bodied ground the pen-drawn lines trace out the hieroglyphs of tree, houses, plants, hillocks, stars, bird, child and ladders. Klee himself refers several times to the tree as the symbol of his creative activity: the tree with its roots sunk into the ground, its sap mounting upwards, its sturdy trunk and concentric rings, its branches reaching out in every direction, its heavenward aspiration. There was a period in his work when, as here, he surrounded his watercolours with thick bands of colour.

Portal of a Mosque is Klee's homage to the Moslem world as he saw it during his trips to Tunisia (1914) and Egypt (1928-1929). This sheet belongs to his divisionist phase of 1931-1932. To vitalize the picture surface with a heightened intensity of pure colour, which he considered "the irrational element of painting," Klee adopted a system of tightly patterned dabs of colour which recalls the method of Seurat and the Neo-Impressionists, but also the fragmentation of Byzantine mosaics. While in Italy in 1926 he had visited Ravenna and marvelled at the mosaics.

After leaving the Bauhaus in 1925, where he had been a colleague of Klee and Kandinsky, Feininger withdrew to the Baltic village of Deep in Pomerania. There he painted some of his finest watercolours of the sea and ships.

94

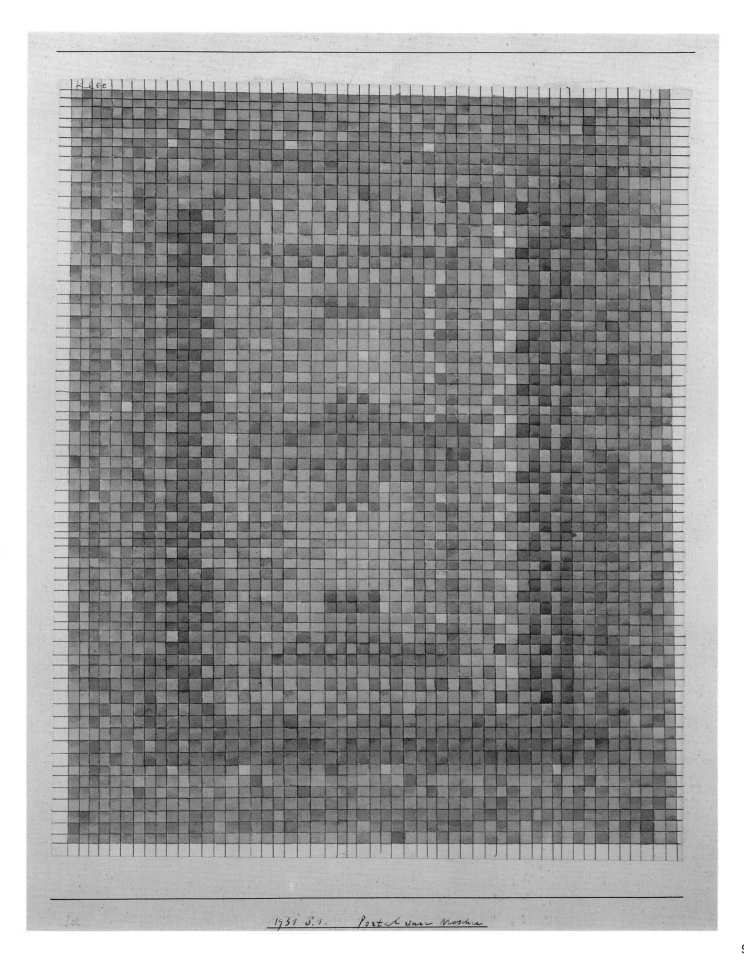

1931 J.1. Portal einer Moschee

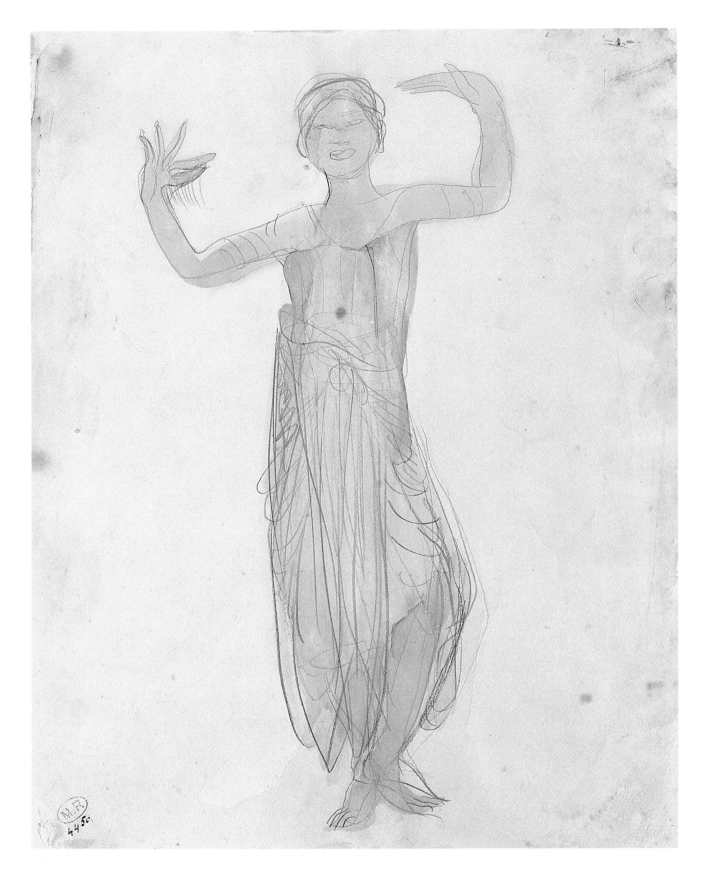

Auguste Rodin
(1840-1917)
Cambodian Dancer, 1906.
Pencil and watercolour
heightened with gouache.

Expressionism and Intimism 9

Two major sculptors in France also painted some highly original watercolours. One was the animal sculptor Barye, a friend of Delacroix's. He studied the wild animals in the zoo cages at the Jardin des Plantes, Paris, and in spirited watercolours imagined them roaming freely in the heath country around Fontainebleau. The other was Rodin, a contemporary of the Impressionists, whose own bent was rather towards Symbolism which he quickened with his exceptional vitality. The watercolour sketches of moving nudes which he multiplied after 1890 prove his sovereign mastery of the medium. They are not preparatory studies but self-contained works of art, a relaxation from his sculptures and in fact, as he said himself, an outcome of them. The best dancers of the day posed in Rodin's studio, and in July 1906 he was captivated by the royal troupe of Cambodian dancers: "Between two pilgrimages to Chartres I went to see the Cambodian dancers. I had already studied them assiduously, both in Paris (at the Pré-Catalan) and in Marseilles (at the Villa des Glycines), with the paper on my knees and pencil in hand, marvelling at their beauty and the distinctive character of their dancing. Till then I knew nothing of this Far Eastern art, and what astonished and delighted me was to rediscover in it the very principle of antique art."

For definite reasons, its primitive organic nature, its provocative or sublimated eroticism, its aerial magic bound by the strictest technique, dancing had a magnetic attraction for modern artists at the turn of the century. Many names could be cited besides that of Rodin. Reproduced here are two opposing versions of this theme, one by Rouault, the other by Derain, both focused on the female figure. Fauvism, igniting the flat picture surface in a blaze of pure colour generating space and light, brought with it a corresponding simplification and tautness of line. Apart from Matisse, who seldom ventured on it except in his Pointillist phase and, as it happens, in a few studies for his 1910 mural composition The Dance, all the Fauve painters, Marquet and Dufy in particular, took up watercolour with enthusiasm. It was also a favourite medium with more traditional artists like Dunoyer de Segonzac and the Belgian colourist Rik Wouters. During the momentous years when he acted as the catalyzing agent between Matisse and Picasso, Derain painted with a fine economy of means his magnificent watercolours of dancers and bathers, conceived, in his own words, as "forms born of the open air, of the bright sunlight and called upon to reveal themselves in bright sunlight."

Rouault exhibited with the Fauves and had been their fellow student in Gustave Moreau's studio in the 1890s, but stylistically, in his emotional vehemence and moral indignation, he stood apart from them. He represents the Christian night-side of Fauvism as radically as his friend Matisse represents its pagan sunny side. Up to 1914 the mixed watercolour, from which Rouault drew a wide range of at once sumptuous and dramatic accents, was the essential vehicle of his religious faith and social crusade.

In Scandinavia and Germany the Norwegian painter Edvard Munch had the same importance as Cézanne in France, and the destiny of modern art gravitated around these two poles. One of Munch's most significant paintings, finished in 1900 and dedicated to the round dance of desire, the gyration of couples, is the Dance of Life. In 1896, during one of several stays in Paris, following up Lautrec and Gauguin, he mastered the techniques of lithography and woodcut and went on to produce a large body of graphic work of high quality, bringing together in concentrated form the repertory of his obsessions. The existential violence and hysteria of his overwrought temperament were crystallized and released in arresting visionary images. Watercolour was well suited to his fluid brushwork and strange northern light.

Munch is the founder of modern Expressionism as manifested first of all at Dresden in 1905 in the art group known as the Brücke (Bridge), headed by Kirchner and including Heckel, Schmidt-Rottluff and Pechstein. The connection with Paris and French Fauvism was made by way of the Dutch painter Kees van Dongen, whose sensuous, provocative watercolours of Montmartre night life figured in the Brücke exhibitions in Dresden. With these German artists, whose strident colours were crossed and contoured by a feverish pattern of lines that revived the old woodcut tradition, the spontaneity of the watercolour technique lent itself readily to their explosive expression of social revolt and animal instincts. By 1911 the focal point of German Expressionism had shifted from Dresden to Berlin, where after the war it was turned into the trenchant realism illustrated by Dix, Grosz and Beckmann, who used watercolour as an instrument of unrelenting satire. Nolde, at their invitation, joined the Brücke group in 1906, but soon went his own way. By temperament he was a solitary and a mystic, in this resembling Rouault in France. Of all the painters of this century, Nolde is probably the one who devoted himself to watercolour most wholeheartedly and most fruitfully. It was his personal path of fulfilment. After 1926, when his graphic work ceases, his watercolours rise to their point of highest intensity in flower pieces. His friend Christian Rohlfs drew mysterious, evanescent effects from watercolour towards the end of his life, in the 1920s and '30s.

In Vienna the master of Jugendstil, Gustav Klimt, used for his subtle erotic evocations the colour crayons that were beginning to be manufactured industrially. His power of line brought its influence to bear on the tormented style of the two foremost painters of Viennese Expressionism, Egon Schiele, who died in 1918 at twenty-eight, and Oskar Kokoschka, who used pure watercolour at various times during his long life. Bonnard, as bold in his intimist vein as the Expressionists were in their frenzied one, came under the spell of watercolour late in life, in 1930, while convalescing from an illness, and handled colour here with the same refinement and originality as in his oils.

Georges Rouault
(1871-1958)
Cancan Dancer at the Tabarin
Cabaret, Paris, 1905.
Watercolour and pastel.

André Derain
(1880-1954)
Bacchic Dance, 1906.
Watercolour.

From 1902 to 1914 Rouault concentrated on three themes, continually reconsidered and reinterpreted: prostitutes, judges, and clowns. He usually painted them in a mixed medium of watercolour, heightened with gouache or pastel and retouched with size tempera or oils thinned with turpentine. In the wake of Seurat and Toulouse-Lautrec, but in wholly personal terms, with a dramatic power all his own, he depicts here the cancan dancer in a Paris cabaret, the Tabarin, then famous for this kind of dancing. The steady jigging of the body, the stamping of the feet, the outflung leg high in the air, all these movements charged with sexual provocation are rendered by rapid, discontinuous, interacting lines and a rich wash of ultramarine delicately varied with pink and black—a colour scheme often likened to that of Picasso's Blue Period, contemporary with this work, but deriving rather from Cézanne and Romanesque stained-glass windows.

The bacchic dance executed in the open air according to the ancient pagan rites is a very different thing from the cabaret turn done by drab dancing girls who make a hard-earned living out of it. During their summer stay together in 1905 at Collioure, a French fishing port at the foot of the eastern Pyrenees, Matisse and Derain rediscovered in the Mediterranean sunlight the classical themes of the pastoral and the bacchanal, which they interpreted in terms of pure colour, with a racy vitality and momentum. Here the elongated forms of the dancers are suggested by a few pliant pencil strokes, while the white of the cream-tinted paper conveys the luminous substance of the figures. They are combined with the romantic motif of trees and leafage. Welling up with a primal, Dionysiac freshness, the colours are patterned in gay complementary harmonies of red and green, and orange and blue.

Egon Schiele
(1890-1918)
Seated Nude, 1910.
Black chalk and watercolour.

Egon Schiele's nudes are as tense and desolate as his land-scapes. Using watercolour washes, he drew the angular contours of the human body with a characteristic emphasis on its painful contortions and erotic torments. "I'm a man, I love death and I love life," wrote Schiele, perhaps with a presentiment of his own untimely death. His style and tem-perament are well conveyed by the staccato phrases of his diary: "Blazes, burns, waves to the struggle—convulsion of mind."
Most of Nolde's watercolours are landscapes and seascapes whose deep-toned colours pulse with the elemental forces of earth, water and sky. Many too are luxuriant evocations of the flowers he grew in his North German garden at See-büll, on the Danish frontier. "Flowers," he liked to say, "make a man blossom into joy." During the darkest years of the war, from 1941 on, when he was forbidden to paint by the Hitler regime, he secretly made the small, fantastic watercolours which he called his "unpainted pictures."

Oskar Kokoschka
(1886-1980)
The Lunatic Girl, c. 1909.
Pencil and watercolour.

This watercolour drawing is an early work by Kokoschka, when he was still under the lingering influence of Gustav Klimt. It is one of a series of psychological portraits done in the stimulating pre-war Vienna of Freud and Musil and Karl Kraus, of the architect Adolf Loos and the composer Arnold Schönberg. Kokoschka had the gift of double vision, the hallucinating knack of penetrating the outward mask and going straight to the psychic heart of his sitters, recording the wry vulnerability of human beings beset by troubles or fears or as here, despite the preciosity of the costume, by lunacy. "It is the business of the creative artist," he wrote, "to identify and define what darkens the spirit of man, then to set that spirit free." Later Kokoschka used pure water-colour, without any underdrawing, for many landscapes, still lifes and figure studies.

Emil Nolde
(1867-1956)

Calla, Anemones and Gerbera.
Watercolour.

◄ **Edvard Munch**
(1863-1944)
Standing Blue Nude, 1920.
Watercolour.

Pierre Bonnard ►
(1867-1947)
Nude by the Tub, 1930-1935.
Watercolour and gouache.

During the many stays he made in Paris between 1885 and 1914, Munch may well have met Bonnard (though there is no actual record of such a meeting), for the two painters moved in the same circles. Both spent many evenings at the Théâtre de l'Œuvre, where Ibsen's plays were performed; both were friends of Thadée Natanson, editor of the *Revue Blanche*, the leading artistic and literary fortnightly in Paris during the 1890s, which at an interval of a few months published articles on Munch and Bonnard. Munch was also a friend of Strindberg, and his early work, like that of the Swedish playwright, offers a terrifying vision of woman as witch or vampire. After his nervous breakdown and its cure in 1909, Munch's mind seemed more at peace with itself and he turned a more objective eye on the outside world. In 1916 he purchased a quiet old house at Ekely, near Oslo, where he lived till his death in 1944. There he made many figure studies, some of them luminous watercolours, from young models in his studio, whom he recorded in a serener, more contemplative mood than in younger days, but responsive as always to their feminine charm.

This Bonnard watercolour heightened with gouache, whose orange and violet tones contrast with the blue contours of Munch's figure study, is one of many sketches for the magnificent oil painting of 1931. From 1908 to the end of his life Bonnard turned again and again, almost obsessively, to this theme of a woman in or by her bathtub. His iridescent nudes, shown in close-up along a plunging line of sight, have nothing of the odalisque, nothing of Oriental exoticism; they are actual bodies, absorbed in their ablutions in the seclusion of the bathroom, and as such they bring to mind the nudes of the Venetian masters and those, too, of Hellenistic statuary.

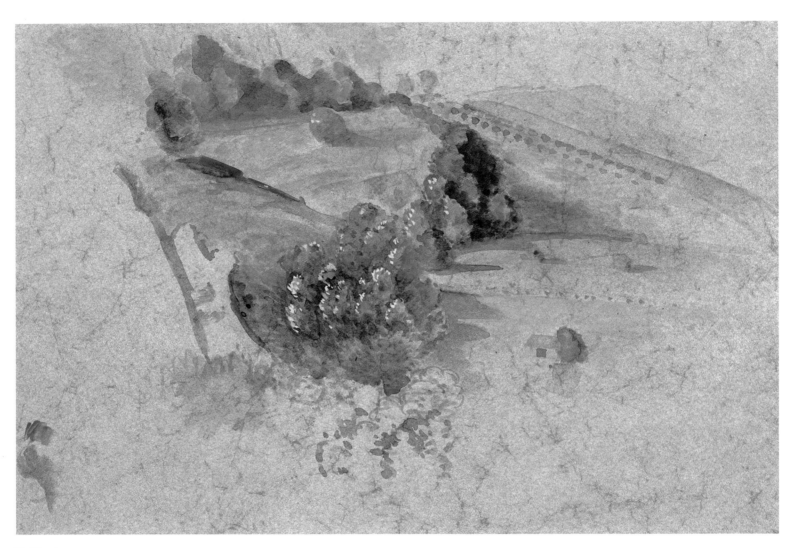

Balthus
(1912)
Landscape at Monte Calvello, c. 1972.
Watercolour.

From Surrealism to Informal Art 10

The relations between painting and drawing, and indeed the very nature of both, have been radically changed in the twentieth century by the invention of new procedures like collage, assemblage, cutout, folding, projection, transfer, automatic writing; also by the development of abstract art which handles line and colour as independent, self-contained elements, as so many non-representational shapes and patterns. The extension of gouache, colour crayons and mixed techniques, and the revival of pastel (all these media being easily reworked and well suited to an age of intense experimentation), together with the proliferation of printmaking, have been detrimental to watercolour, which may be said to have reached its peak in the nineteenth century. Watercolour is still practised, but its focus has shifted from the outward to the inward landscape, to what Henri Michaux has called "the spaces of the inner man."

Dada responded to the senseless slaughter of the First World War by an outburst of nihilism and sardonic humour. Surrealism, which followed it up, was animated by poets and literary men: unlike Cubism, it was not a revolution of form but an adventure of the mind in quest of the marvellous, tapping the unconscious sources of creation. Miró and Chagall both favoured gouache. Of the other painters of these two movements who used watercolour inventively in combination with collage, Francis Picabia, Max Ernst and André Masson stand out. Surrealism aimed at unusual imagery, but its radical ferment and psychic automatism reactivated by the shock of the Second World War contributed to the rise of Abstract Expressionism in the United States and Informal Art in Europe—that is, a new way of painting in which art and life are not divided, in which substance and content coincide, in which the upsurge of the sign precedes its signification. During his initial biomorphic phase, Jackson Pollock experimented with a ground mixture of gouache and pastel, then came the sweeping gesture and drip technique, applied to large canvases laid flat on the floor, in which he engrossed himself totally. In France the informal painters kept to small formats and, following up Klee's work, went on to do non-figurative watercolours: Wols, who stands unique and apart in his existential trance and poetic animism; Bryen, whose colour-light particles arise in lyrical vitality from an inner realm and quiver in the sun; and Michaux, fascinated by lines and signs, for whom painting is at once exorcism and ecstasy, a throwing off of inertia, a reaching out to the "trans-real."

While the pioneers of American painting, like Winslow Homer and John Marin, and later major figures like Charles Demuth, Georgia O'Keeffe and Edward Hopper, did some of their finest work in watercolour, the New York School of the 1940s and its aftercomers ignored watercolour for aesthetic and material reasons, in particular because of the large formats they used and their all-over technique. Such was the colour-field painting of Newman and Rothko. A significant exception is Helen Frankenthaler, who went through a watercolour period before working out her own technique of soaking and staining paint directly into the raw unprimed canvas: her colour abstractions, developed with her on large surfaces by Noland, Morris Louis and Olitski, have the freshness and immediacy of watercolour. The Pacific Coast painters who visited the Far East and steeped themselves in Oriental philosophies, like Morris Graves and Mark Tobey, or who looked to Europe, like Tobey again and Sam Francis, found watercolour an apt and satisfying medium. The Canadian J. P. Riopelle has given watercolour a preponderant place in the development of his monumental, richly textured work. Hartung at the age of eighteen, in 1922, painted some extraordinary watercolours, which are like a foretaste of *tachisme*, but in his mature style there was no place for watercolour. The same is true of the textural painters and the gestural painters who, like him, build up space in terms of dark, clustered signs.

Some painters of the School of Paris prefer gouache (Poliakoff, Vieira da Silva); others have practised watercolour for its fine chromatic purity at necessary moments of their career (Bazaine, Estève, Manessier). For Estève, each technique calls for so exclusive a concentration that he has to give up oil painting when he turns to watercolours. The Chinese painter Zao Wou-Ki, who has an instinctive love and mastery of the monochrome wash, has filled several sketchbooks with spare, refined watercolours done in the course of his painting trips through France, Spain and Italy. The Czech painter Sima, who also lived in Paris, and a close friend of Jouve and Michaux, cuts his sharp-edged light effects out of the crystal of a subtle geometry, using two tones of ochre and blue. In Italy, where it occurs intermittently in the work of abstract colourists like Afro, Santomaso, Corpora and Dorazio, the figurative watercolour has been handled with dazzling virtuosity by de Pisis and Guttuso, with an intimacy and restraint all his own by Morandi, with discriminating ardour by Music. In England, where abstraction has remained marginal, the landscape tradition of watercolour has been maintained by many artists of talent, but with no dominant personality among them; most memorable and poignant are Henry Moore's watercolour drawings of civilians huddled together in the London Tube shelters in 1940-1942. Two outstanding watercolourists in Germany are Ernst Wilhelm Nay, following in the steps of Munch and Nolde, and Julius Bissier, inspired by Far Eastern art.

Balthus stands apart. He is an artist who has sought to revive a lost beauty and forgotten secrets of craftsmanship. He draws with a velvety pencil the figures of adolescent girls asleep, daydreaming or absorbed in reading and paints in watercolour still lifes and landscapes which combine his personal sensibility with Cézannian structure and Chinese delicacy. To young painters willing to return to the poetry of reality and the magic of watercolour, Balthus offers not a model but an example.

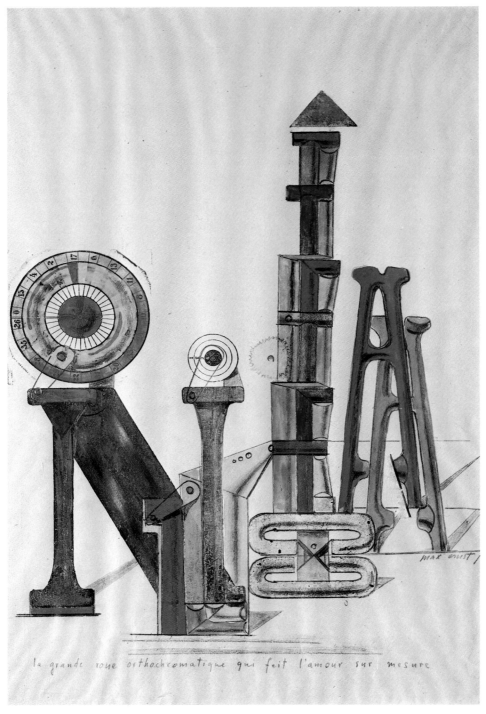

la grande roue orthochromatique qui fait l'amour sur mesure

Max Ernst
(1891-1976)

The Great Orthochromatic Wheel
Which Makes Love to Measure, 1919.
Pencil and watercolour over printed sheets.

▲ **André Masson**
(1896)
Matador Insects, 1941.
Pen and watercolour.

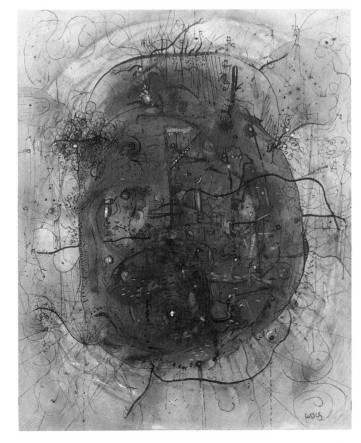

▼ **Wols**
(1913-1951)
Composition, c. 1946.
Pen and watercolour.

This watercolour of 1919, done on printed sheets, belongs to the series of drawings and collages inspired by the advertisements in a printed catalogue illustrating objects of scientific research. Max Ernst's "excited gaze" was provoked by those pages: "Here I discover the elements of a figuration so remote that its very absurdity provokes in me a sudden intensification of my faculties of sight." The whimsical caption he added heightens the discrepancy between the original mechanical image and the erotic subversion of it contrived by the artist.

A draughtsman whose hand was continually set moving by what he saw or imagined, André Masson painted several taut and vivid watercolours of insects, soon after his arrival in the United States in 1941. They are a belated echo of his years in Spain (1934-1936). "I have made some bullfighting pictures with insects," he wrote. "These little insects facing an animal straight out of prehistory. They aroused my imagination, and I saw in them all sorts of things."

Taking up where Surrealism and Klee left off, Wols developed his art in solitude during the war, while a refugee in France at Cassis (Riviera), then at Dieulefit (Drôme). The outflow of unconscious associations is like an animist fusion with nature. "At Cassis the stones, fish and rocks, the sea brine and the sky, made me forget the importance of man, urged me to turn my back on the chaos of his doings, and showed me eternity in the lapping wavelets of the port, ever repeated without repeating themselves. Nothing can be fathomed, all we know is appearances. All loves lead to one. Over and above personal loves is nameless love."

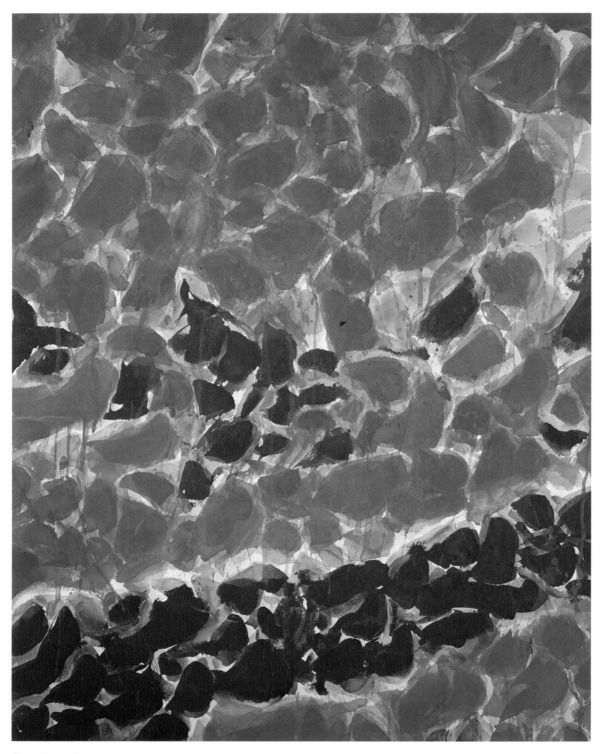

Sam Francis
(1923)
Untitled Watercolour, 1954.

"Space in the painting of Sam Francis develops out of a maze of forms which always lead the eye on to fresh discoveries. He seems to take a peculiar delight in abandoning himself to the adventure of the moment, as his hand and brush trace out its devious path. And his delight seems to reach its peak in an exhilarating shower of colour cascading over the whole surface of the picture, sparkling with vagrant lights, with transparent eddies of blue, red and yellow. This art exemplifies the modern will to participate in the life of the painting itself, in the vibrant glitter of the colours. Appearances notwithstanding, these colours are not a pictorial transposition of naturalistic lighting... These are inward colours, never without a certain tremulous delicacy even when in the grip of emphatic textural rhythms and fragmented forms" (Nello Ponente).

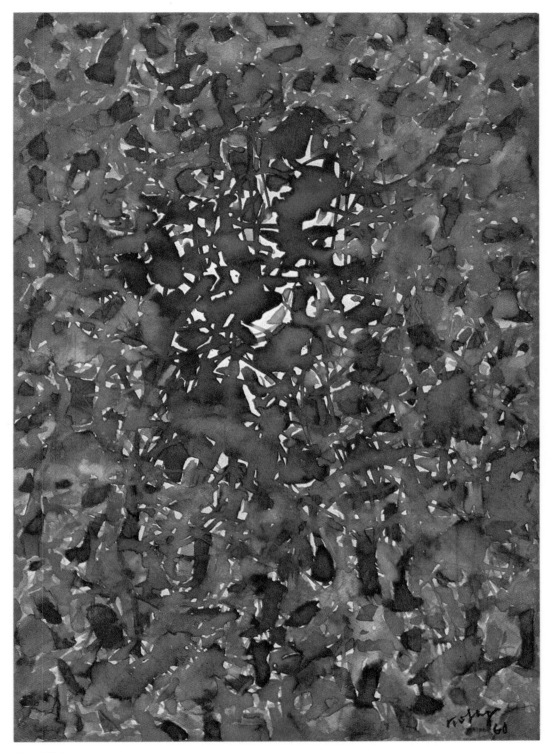

Mark Tobey
(1890-1976)
Enchanted Garden, 1960.
Watercolour.

Tobey grew up in Wisconsin and Indiana: "My whole early experience until I was sixteen was just purely nature. Not the mind at all, just nature." In 1927 he settled in Seattle, which remained his home until 1960, when he moved to Basel, Switzerland, attracted by its humanistic tradition. Throughout his life Tobey owed much to the stimulus of places: Chicago and New York, where he was trained and converted to the Baha'i faith; China and Japan, where he steeped himself in Zen and Oriental calligraphy and developed his natural "writing impulse"; and England, where he lived from 1931 to 1938 at Dartington Hall in Devon, working out his characteristic "white writing" style and moving in a circle of artists and writers that included Pearl Buck, Arthur Waley, Aldous Huxley and Rabindranath Tagore, intent like Tobey on a fusion of East and West.

Hans Hartung
(1904)
Yellow, Red and Blue, 1922.
Watercolour.

The premonitory watercolours made in 1922 by the young Hans Hartung, when he was still a schoolboy in Dresden, consist of bright colours, here the three primary tones, splashed over the paper, and the speed of gesture they already vouch for became an essential part of his later equipment as a painter. Estève's watercolours, on the contrary, grow from a slow, deliberate overlaying of cool and warm tones which imparts a rich density to the transparent movements of light. Plenitude of colour is inseparable for him from the sound construction of form and the architectonic rhythm of space. Estève has never forgotten the rural freedom and emotions of his childhood in the Berry region of central France: this remains the vital source of his art. "But as a painter," he writes, "I feel nature more intensely through the forms I discover than through the world I live in."

Maurice Estève
(1904)
Watercolour No. 995 A, 1968.

110

Jean-Paul Riopelle
(1923)
Composition, 1961.
Watercolour.

"For me," says Riopelle, "nature is the only reference. Only there does freedom exist and at the same time the strongest constraint. A tree can only grow in one way. There is no tragic or elegiac or joyful way of being a tree. There is only the right way." When the group of watercolours to which this one belongs was exhibited in 1962 at the National Gallery of Canada in Ottawa, the critic Guy Viau wrote: "This very fine series of watercolours is certainly a revelation. Their composition is very peculiar: between the picture space and us it throws up a barbed wire fence, a network of sharp and delicate patterns through which stretch the distances containing all the light in the picture. They are swept up by two contending forces: a dominant of verticals tending towards a void where light rushes in, then an unexpected, indefinable gravitation which restores the balance."

Giorgio Morandi
(1890-1964)
Still Life.
Watercolour on cardboard.

Joseph Sima
(1891-1971)
Untitled Watercolour, 1960.

Julius Bissier
(1893-1965)
9 Nov. 61.
Watercolour.

Antonio Zoran Music
(1909)
Untitled Watercolour, 1983.

"Paper that drinks in the paint, greedily, persistently, deeply, that's what appeals to me more than colours, which as a matter of fact I just fling on it as baits, as revealers, as loose, untidy masses. Usually and most naturally I put on some red. After all, what spreads more easily than blood?

"Water paints, broad as a lake, water the all-swallowing demon, drowner of islands, maker of mirages, breaker of dams, the world-overflower... I see with at first a secret but then an ever more undisguised joy this outflow of line from my design, into the water, and the infiltration spreading everywhere" (Henri Michaux).

Jean Bazaine
(1904)
Untitled Watercolour, 1975.

Zao Wou-Ki
(1921)
Saint-Jeoire-en-Faucigny, 1950.
Watercolour.

Henri Michaux
(1899)
Untitled Watercolour, 1970.

114

Camille Bryen
(1907-1977)
No. 554, 1961.
Watercolour.

''I began to draw for drawing's sake, for living's sake, wordlessly, thoughtlessly. First sprang up walls of paper which surrounded me from head to foot with transhuman anatomies and cannibalistic metaphors. I passed through realms, I was a miner, I was a crow.

''Then these spaces were eaten or drunk. Mosaics of colour patches and signs, and I became a building, a tunnel. Muscles dripped with juice, tubes lit up and wrapped over the inexplicable. No representation, no meaning, no control, just a style of being, a sharing in gestures and things airing the human and the non-human. The painting looked at me, its eye at the keyhole. The eye is facing me, the canvas is an open mirror'' (Camille Bryen).

Colours soluble in water, mixed with gum arabic, honey, sugar or other substances, were already known to the Egyptians in the twelfth century B.C. In ancient China, too, such colours were applied to fabrics. In Europe during the Middle Ages water paints were used in the illumination of vellum manuscripts, and Cennino Cennini describes the technique of watercolour painting in his Libro dell'Arte *(c. 1400). The first books on the subject appeared in England in the later seventeenth century.*

The making of watercolour paints today, described here by Peter Staples of Winsor & Newton, is the outcome of this long tradition.

Half-tube of crimson lake

Artists' watercolours are suspensions of finely ground, strongly coloured pigments evenly dispersed in an aqueous gum solution. They are made primarily to be applied to good quality white watercolour paper in thin washes and are essentially transparent colours which use the luminosity of the white paper to show through the transparent washes, thus enhancing the brilliance of the colours. It is this transparency which separates artists' watercolours from designers' gouache or poster colour which are both essentially opaque when brushed out, completely obliterating the underlying surface. Transparency is achieved by a higher proportion of media to pigment in the finished colour. This higher gum content enables watercolours to be applied in highly diluted washes without any

Cake of watercolour paint

tendency for the pigment to rub off the surface of the paper.

Watercolours dry solely by the evaporation of the water content and the dried paint films are easily resoluble in water. It is this very property which makes this method of painting so demanding. Artists' watercolours are now sold in two forms, in metal collapsible tubes and in pans.

The Media

The best watercolours use several types of gum. The selection of the best combination of gums is determined by trial and error, finding out which gum or gums combine best with an individual pigment or pigment combination, by making small trial batches. The basic gum used at Winsor & Newton Ltd for their artists' watercolours is a pale gum arabic imported from the Sudan. A tree resin, gum arabic is crushed down to a fine powder and then made into a gum solution by stirring it into hot water. When cooled, the gum solution is strained to remove all impurities and a preservative is added. For certain pigment

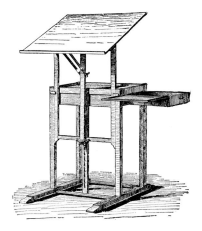

Watercolourist's studio table

types, such as ultramarine which is sensitive to acids, the basic gum solution is modified by neutralizing its acidic properties with the addition of borax and glycerine. With other pigments, such as alizarin crimson, better dispersion is achieved with an addition of a pale aqueous dextrine solution which is a potato starch product.

Heavy pigments sometimes require the medium to be thickened so that separation in the tube does not occur; this can be achieved with careful additions of gum tragacanth or arrowroot. Gum tragacanth is also used to improve the plasticity of certain moist pan colours (e.g. cadmium yellow or Chinese white).

Glycerine is added because of its hydrophilic (water-seeking) properties. The Winsor & Newton partnership was formed in 1832 soon after the discovery of glycerine and the founders of the Company were the first to use its hydrophilic properties to help the moist pans of watercolour to release colour when wetted with a brush. Without glycerine a good deal of scrubbing was required before the colour was released from the old cake colours which preceded the moist pans. But excess glycerine will attract moisture from the air and make pan colours sticky and even paintings tacky.

Most pigments are not soluble in water, and therefore wetting agents are added to the media to improve the wetting and aid the dispersion. The most successful wetting agent is refined ox gall, and for pale colours (e.g. cadmium yellow pale) clarified ox gall. Other wetting agents are commercially available for improving the dispersion of individual pigments; again only trial and error will give the best answer. Some pigments when dispersed in gum solutions will give a gelatinous structure to the paint which will not brush out smoothly; solutions of potassium citrate or potassium tartrate will help to cure this problem.

Without preservatives gum solutions will start growing mould in a week or two. So great care has to be taken to prevent mould growth in all possible climatic conditions, from equatorial to antarctic. One of Winsor & Newton's prize possessions is a letter received from Captain Wilson on Scott's ill-fated bid to be first to reach the South Pole, describing "how well his colours were standing up to that extreme climate." The main preservatives used are dilute aqueous solutions of phenol and formaldehyde. For the very best watercolours all solutions are made with pure distilled water, for tap water contains calcium and magnesium salts which can form

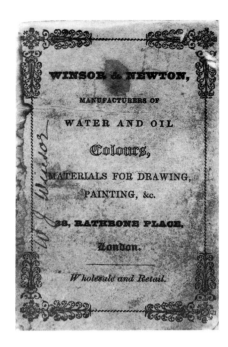

COLOURS

PREPARED IN SPIRITS, IN IMPALPABLE POWDER, FOR OIL OR WATER COLOUR PAINTING; ALSO IN BLADDERS, FINELY GROUND IN OIL.

Ultramarine	Vermillion
Ultramarine Ashes	Flake White
French Ultramarine	Nottingham ditto
Carmine	Silver ditto
Rose Madder	Blue Black
Pink ditto	Brown Ochre
Purple ditto	Burnt Umber
Brown ditto	Burnt Sienna
Crimson Lake	Chrome Yellow
Scarlet ditto	Cologne Earth
Purple ditto	Emerald Green
Indian ditto	Ivory Black
Pure Scarlet	King's Yellow
Cobalt Blue	Lamp Black
Smalt	Light Red
Lemon Yellow	Naples Yellow
Yellow Lake	Patent ditto
Italian Pink	Raw Sienna
Brown ditto	Raw Umber
Verdigrise	Roman Ochre
Prussian Blue	Terra Verte
Antwerp ditto	Vandyke Brown
Indigo	Venetian Red
Bone Brown	Yellow Ochre
Indian Red	

The French Mars Colours.

In 1832 William Winsor and H. C. Newton founded their company for the manufacture of water and oil colours and painters' materials, doing business at 38 Rathbone Place, London. Their first catalogue lists the colours available.

Water bottle

cloudy layers on a watercolour wash and affect the fine dispersions of certain pigments.

Pigments

Nearly all known pigments are suitable for use as watercolours (some have a tendency to be rather gritty, e.g. viridian). Lead white is one that is not used, as it has problems which do not occur with the much preferred Chinese white (zinc oxide). Winsor & Newton currently have 87 colours on their list. They are classified into 24 extremely permanent colours, amongst them the earth colours which include a beautifully transparent shade of burnt sienna, metallic salts such as cerulean blue, viridinia, and ivory black made from calcined animal bones; and 48 durable colours, including cadmium yellow and rose madder, a colour now unique to Winsor & Newton, extracted from the root of the plant Rubius Tinctoras. For applications when durability is not of great priority, there are 9 moderately durable colours and 6 fugitive colours.

Manufacture

The first operation is to check that all of the raw materials are pure and up to specification. The gums are checked for paleness and clarity; many pigments have extra washes in distilled water to ensure freedom from soluble salts; and the various wetting agents, preservatives, and even the distilled water are regularly checked for impurities.

Each colour has its own individual tailored formulation, many largely unaltered for a hundred years, and its own individual method of manufacture (e.g. vermilion). The pigment is added to the media, often by hand with a wooden paddle; batch sizes may only be a few gallons at a time. The mixing is the first part of the dispersion process, the aim of which is firstly to break up all aggregates of pigment, and secondly to grind the pigment to a desired particle size, and lastly to envelope each pigment particle with a coating of the medium. In the Middle Ages the master artist would employ an apprentice to mix and grind his colours, probably on a smooth slab of granite, with a heavy granite muller about the size of a bowler hat; he would grind the colour for hours on end. Some hand mulling is still necessary, where particular colours can be damaged by over grinding (e.g. vermilion). But most colours can be safely dispersed on a three-roll granite mill which squeezes the paint between rollers revolving in opposite directions.

The colour is ladled onto granite slabs some of which are cold for the sensitive colours (e.g. permanent rose and lemon yellow). Some are warm (e.g. for alizarin crimson), and some are hot (e.g. for cobalt blue and lamp black). The colour destined for filling into tubes is left in the drying room for a short time until the consistency is just right. Colour destined for pan colour stays longer in the drying room until it has the consistency of stiff nougat. Another wash is made of the pan colour to ensure that the colour and flow has not changed during the drying

Sunshade

process. The colour is then extruded into strips and guillotined into the correct size to be fitted into plastic pans.

Peter Staples
Technical Director
Winsor & Newton, London

The vignettes are reproduced from *La Peinture à l'Aquarelle. A l'Atelier et sur Nature*, Paris, c. 1910.

A Florentine painter in the tradition of Giotto, Cennino Cennini wrote a craftsman's handbook, Il Libro dell'Arte (c. 1400), giving detailed information about the painting techniques in use in his time. It has been aptly described as "medieval in its encyclopaedic scope and approach, modern in its insistence on the innovations of Giotto."

Chapter XXXI
How you should draw and paint on paper tinted with watercolours, and then heighten it with white lead.
When your hand is practised in shading, take a small brush and with watercolour of ink in a saucer lay in the main folds, then shade off the darker side of them. And this watercolour you are using should be almost like faintly stained water, and the brush should always be kept nearly dry. Working slowly, go on shading little by little, always returning with your brush to the darker places. And do you know what will come of this? If the water you are using is but faintly stained and your shading is done with delight, unhurriedly, the shapes you obtain will be graduated like smoke finely shaded off. Take heed to ply the brush always flat against the paper. When you have brought your shading to perfection, put a drop or two of ink on the watercolour and with your brush blend it well. And then, in the way described, work your brush into the depth of these folds, seeking our their hollows, and always keeping in mind the shading of them. This consists of three parts: one part, shade; another, colouring of the field before you; the other, heightening with white. When you have done this, take a small amount of white lead well mixed with gum arabic (further on I shall explain how this gum is to be dissolved and I shall speak of all the temperas): a bit of white lead is enough. Have some clear water in a saucer, dip your brush into it, then rub your brush over this white lead ground up in a saucer, but rub it thoroughly if the white lead has dried. Then use the palm of your hand or your thumb to press and squeeze the brush, removing the water from it and almost drying it. And begin, holding it flat, to rub the brush over and in those places where whiteness and relief are wanted; and go over them several times with your brush, plying it with feeling. Then, for the extremities of the parts in relief, where they project most strongly, take a pointed brush and apply white lead to them with the tip of the brush and tone up the intensity of the whites. Then with a small brush and pure ink tone up the folds and contours, the noses and eyes, and the down of hair and beards.

Chapter XXXII
How you can whiten with watercolour of white lead, just as you can shade with watercolour of ink.
When you are more practised, I urge you to go on and heighten your shapes perfectly with watercolours, just as you do with watercolour of ink. Take the white lead ground up with water and mix it with egg yolk, and use it for shading off just as you do with watercolour of ink. But this is more difficult for you to manage, and more practice will be wanted. Such is the technique of drawing on tinted paper, and this is the way that will lead you to the art of colouring. Follow it as best you can, for it is the sum and substance of what you must learn. Set yourself to it diligently, and you will take pleasure and delight in it.

About 1750, in Les Règles du Dessin et du Lavis, *the French engineer Buchotte described the preparation of water paints.*

Carmine, ultramarine, vermilion and Prussian blue are dispersed in a gum arabic solution, by stirring them with the finger-tip in a small china saucer or in shells, care being taken for both finger-tip and bowl to be neither greasy nor dirty. But carmine and ultramarine are rather dear, and what clings to the finger-tip is so much lost paint. Therefore, to mix these two colours, I use a small stick of ivory, flat at both ends, one end being used for the crimson, the other for the ultramarine.

In 1776, at the Paris Salon, appeared the word "aquarella," described as "a new kind of painting."

Paul Sandby (1730-1809) has been called the founder of English watercolour painting, and this charming composition of his (c. 1770, Royal Library, Windsor Castle) shows an amateur watercolourist at work, at an artist's table, with her paints set out in rows of oyster shells.

In 1791 the word "aquarelle" appeared for the first time in French, in the one-volume Encyclopédie Méthodique *published that year by Panckoucke in Paris. The article "Aquarelle" describes the watercolour technique:*

Wash drawing in which different colours are used, forming a kind of painting without impasto which might better be described as illumination. The colours here are transparent, devoid of any thickness. It is therefore necessary, for this kind of work, to choose those colours which have least body or to remove the body from those which have any. They should be not so much colours as tints. See the article Bistre for the process of removing body from colours. Paints derived from flowers have no body and are suitable for watercolour. See the article Sunflower for the manner of pressing tinctures out of flowers.

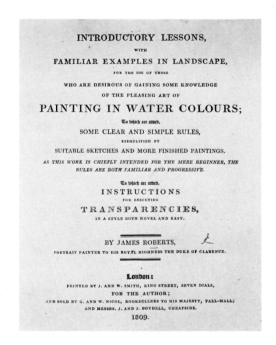

Title page of
James Roberts' book
Painting in Water Colours,
London, 1809.

The popularity of watercolour painting was such, in early nineteenth-century England, that many technical and theoretical books were published on the subject.

They were preceded, in the latter half of the eighteenth century, by several essays on the aesthetics of landscape painting, in particular those of Alexander Cozens, *A New Method of Assisting the Invention in Drawing Original Compositions of Landscape* (1784) and William Gilpin, *Observations relative chiefly to Picturesque Beauty* (1785). As early as 1732 had appeared an anonymous treatise, *The Art of Drawing and Painting in Water-Colours*, printed for J. Peele, London. Two other books with the same title were published, one anonymously in 1770, the other by J. Payne in 1797. From 1796 to 1841 Rudolph Ackermann published a series of handbooks; for example, *Superfine Water Colours* in 1801.
Many English artists wrote about the technique of watercolour painting. John Varley, as both teacher and practising artist, published a *Treatise on the Principles of Landscape Design* (1816-1821), *Precepts of Landscape Drawing* (1818) and *Observations on Colouring... from Nature* (1830), among other writings which take up and amplify the ideas of Thomas Girtin. Varley's friend, the painter and theorist Francis Nicholson, published *The Practice of Drawing and Painting Landscapes from Nature* (1820). Constable in his lifetime published *Various Subjects of Landscape, characteristic of English Scenery* (1830-1832, reissued in 1855 as *English Landscape Scenery*); his *Correspondence* (6 volumes, 1962-1968) and *Discourses* (1970) have now been published in full. Other writings of note are those of David Cox, *Treatise on Landscape Painting* (1814) and *The Young Artist's Companion* (1825); Samuel Prout, *Rudiments of Landscape in Progressive Studies* (1813) and the series of *Easy Lessons in Landscape Drawing* (1820); and of course the voluminous writings of John Ruskin, in particular *Modern Painters* (5 volumes, 1843-1860).

1804: The Society of Painters in Water-Colours, London.

The Royal Academy of Arts in London was founded in 1768 "for the purpose of cultivating and improving the arts of painting, sculpture and architecture." Painting at that time meant oil painting, and watercolour was thought of as being little more than tinted drawing. After 1791 watercolourists were allowed to take part in the Academy exhibitions at Somerset House, but their work was not hung well or prominently. Therefore, on the evening of 30 November 1804, meeting at the Stratford Coffee House in Oxford Street, they founded their own Society of Painters in Water-Colours (later known as the Old Water-Colour Society). The first of their annual exhibitions opened on 22 April 1805 at 20 (now 54) Lower Brook Street. Lasting for six weeks, it was a great success, nearly 12,000 persons paying the shilling entrance fee.

(For further details, see Martin Hardie, *Water-Colour Painting in Britain*, Vol. II, *The Romantic Period*, Batsford, London, 1967, p. 111ff.)

In 1829 the word "aquarelliste" first appeared in France.

In 1866 the American Watercolor Society was founded in New York. Incorporated in 1903, it merged with the New York Watercolor Club in 1941. Today it has 450 members and holds an annual exhibition in April at the National Academy of Design in New York.

Title page of a handbook on miniature, gouache and watercolour painting, Paris, 1827.

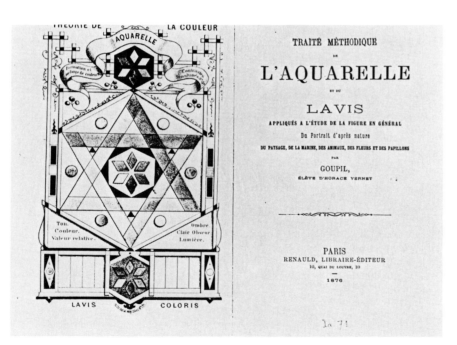

Frontispiece and title page of Goupil's treatise on watercolour and wash, Paris, 1876.

In 1878 the Société des Aquarellistes Français was founded in Paris by J. G. Vibert, its most prominent member being Eugène Lami.

This French watercolour society has held regular exhibitions ever since, first in the Rue Laffitte, Paris, then at the Galerie Georges Petit in the Rue de Sèze.

122

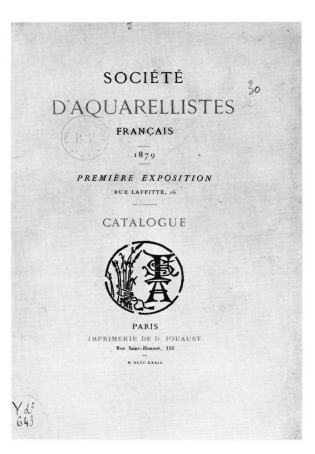

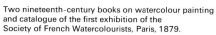

Two nineteenth-century books on watercolour painting
and catalogue of the first exhibition of the
Society of French Watercolourists, Paris, 1879.

EXPOSITION DE LA SOCIÉTÉ DES AQUARELLISTES, RUE DE SÉZE. — Voir le précédent numéro, page 118.

Exhibition of the
Society of French
Watercolourists,
Paris, 1882.

Four working sheets by Paul Signac:

These four small watercolours, with the artist's annotations on the quality of the paper, come from a notebook containing samples of watercolour and drawing paper (size $8\frac{1}{4} \times 9$ in.) from the Van Gelder mill in Amsterdam. Dating from about 1925-1927, these seascapes were painted at the mouth of the Trieux River near Paimpol in Brittany.

(Private Collection, Paris)

un peu lisse +
trop solennel.

S 4
Royaal Vergé
50 × 66 cM. 21 Kg. per 480 vel.

Très Bon   Bonnes teinte.
Bon grain

No. 20
Propatria Velin
35 × 44 cM. 10 Kg. per 500 vel.

Le haut court bien
un peu trop lisse pendt
par l'agua.

No. 1708
Propatria Vergé
35 × 44 cM. 8½ Kg. per 480 vel.

trop torchon — mauvais joue le
trav

S 8 mat
Dubbel Olifants Vergé
68 × 102 cM. 65 Kg. per 480 vel.

A friend of Géricault, with whom he visited England in 1820-1821, Nicolas-Toussaint Charlet (1792-1845) was a keen watercolourist who perfected his technique by working with Bonington; he is best known as an illustrator of the Napoleonic legend. As Professor of Drawing at the Ecole Polytechnique in Paris, Charlet wrote an interesting essay on the watercolour technique:

Watercolour is an agreeable and convenient form of art: agreeable in that it is neither messy nor troublesome, and everything needed to practise it can be carried in a six by four inch box, and so it is ideal for the travelling artist. Add to this box a notebook or pad with sheets of paper, and you are ready for a painting trip in forest or mountains... As a practising watercolourist, perhaps I can give some advice worth having about the handling of water paints. Once your drawing is built up with lines and shaded in, you lay in the broad luminous tones of your sky first of all, then of your background; after that come your foreground, terrain, trees and buildings. But in the name of all you hold dearest, do not try to blend your tones. Where you see purple, put that on; where you see greenish, put that on; likewise with blue and green. Don't lose your nerve if your drawing begins to look like a mosaic or a piece of marquetry. That is all to the good. The important thing is to put your blue and yellow and so on in the right place...

The watercolour painted in the studio or at home can, if skilfully done, vie with oils; it may even be superior in the delicacy of tones in light. But the pitfall is the shadows and chiaroscuro. Since the colour is absorbed by the paper and forms a faint down on the surface, one is often forced to do some rubbing out, and here it is no easy matter to rework one's picture. The best course is to mass one's shadows firmly, always preparing them beforehand with warm and transparent tones; then, when the drawing is almost finished, to glaze it with water slightly mixed with gum, and let it stand.

Camille Pissarro wrote to Paul Signac on 30 August 1888:

I have done a lot of watercolours, which help me to do a picture, and a good many small pastels. I recommend watercolour to you, it is valuable and most useful. In a few minutes one can take down notes unobtainable in any other way, the fluidity of a sky, certain transparencies, a lot of small particulars that a long piece of work cannot give you: these effects are so fleeting...

Paul Signac wrote in his book on Jongkind, published in 1927:

There are no fine tones in watercolour unless one makes play with the white of the paper, not only letting it shine through transparently, but contriving to set it off in varying proportions around each brushstroke. This luminous intermediary intensifies each tone and harmonizes it with the others around it.

If a patch of blue is put down beside a patch of red and the two are brought so close as to touch each other, their meeting will be discordant. If a white space is left between these two hostile tones, they will harmonize, each shading off into the unpainted white, and their reciprocal intensity will be heightened by the contrast with this white surface. These interplays of white with colours are always agreeable to the eye.

Indeed there are some tones that cannot keep their quality unless they are surrounded by white. Yellow and orange become meaningless, lifeless, if the eye cannot compare them with a neighbouring white.

Contrary to the rules, one must have no fear about leaving blank spaces.

Bibliography

List of illustrations

Index of names
and places

Bibliography

G. ADRIANI, *Cézanne, Aquarelles*, Paris, 1984. — J.C. AMMAN, *Louis Moilliet, Das Gesamtwerk*, Cologne, 1972. — A. ANANOFF, *L'œuvre dessiné de Jean-Honoré Fragonard. Catalogue raisonné*, 4 vols., Paris, 1961-1970.

M.L. BATAILLE and G. WILDENSTEIN, *Berthe Morisot, Catalogue des peintures, pastels et aquarelles*, Paris, 1961. — O. BENESCH, *Master Drawings in the Albertina. European Drawings from the 15th to the 18th Century*, Greenwich, Conn., 1967. — K. BERGER, *Géricault and His Work*, Lawrence, Kansas, 1955. — D. BINDMAN, *William Blake. Catalogue of the Collection in the Fitzwilliam Museum*, Cambridge, 1970. — D. BINDMAN, *William Blake. The Complete Graphic Works*, London, 1978. — A. BLUNT, *The Art of William Blake*, London, 1959. — A. BURY, *Water-Colour Painting of Today*, London, 1937. — G. BUSCH, *Die Tunisreise, Aquarelle und Zeichnungen von August Macke*, Cologne, 1958. — M. BUTLIN, *William Blake. A Complete Catalogue of the Works in the Tate Gallery*, London, 1971; *The Paintings and Drawings of William Blake*, 2 vols., London, 1981.

F. CACHIN, *Paul Signac*, Paris, 1971. — G. CARANDENTE, *Balthus: Drawings and Watercolors*, Greenwich, Conn., 1983. — J. CASSOU and J. LEYMARIE, *Fernand Léger: Drawings and Gouaches*, Greenwich, Conn., 1973. — D. CLIFFORD, *Watercolours of the Norwich School*, London, 1965. — R. COGNIAT, *Dessins et aquarelles du XXᵉ siècle*, Paris, 1922. — A. COMINI, *Egon Schiele*, New York, 1976. — D. COOPER, *Drawings and Watercolors by Vincent Van Gogh*, New York, 1955. — D. COX, *A Treatise on Landscape Painting*, London, 1814, reprinted in *The Studio*, special number, London, 1922.

E. DACIER, *Gabriel de Saint-Aubin*, 2 vols., Paris, 1929. — F. DAULTE, *French Watercolours of the 20th Century*, New York and London, 1968; *French Watercolours of the 19th Century*, New York and London, 1969. — B. DORIVAL, *Robert Delaunay*, Paris, 1975.

C. EISLER, *A Treasury of Great Master Drawings*, New York and London, 1975. — L. EITNER, *Géricault: His Life and Work*, New York and London, 1982.

A.J. FINBERG, *The English Watercolourists*, London, 1906; *The Development of British Landscape Painting in Water-Colours*, in *The Studio*, special number, London, 1917-1918. — I. FLEMING-WILLIAMS, *Constable: Landscape Drawings and Watercolours*, London, 1976.

P. GANZ, *The Paintings of Hans Holbein*, London, 1950. — W. GEORGE and G. NOUAILLE-ROUAULT, *Rouault*, London, 1971. — E.H. GOMBRICH, *Norm and Form: Studies in the Art of the Renaissance*, London and New York, 1966. — L. GOODRICH, *Winslow Homer*, New York, 1959. — L. GOWING, *Turner, Imagination and Reality*, London and New York, 1966. — M.H. GRANT, *A Dictionary of British Landscape Painters, from the 16th to the Early 20th Century*, Leigh-on-Sea, 1976. — W. GROHMANN, *Hans Hartung. Aquarelle 1922*, St Gall, Switzerland, 1966 (text in German, French and English). — P. GRUNCHEC, *Tout l'œuvre peint de Géricault*, Paris, 1978; *Géricault, Dessins et aquarelles de chevaux*, Paris, 1982.

M. HARDIE, *Water-Colour Painting in Britain, I The Eighteenth Century, II The Romantic Period, III The Victorian Period*, 3 vols., London, 1966-1968. — C. HAYES, *The Technique of Water-Colour Painting*, London and New York, 1967. — V. HEFTING, *Jongkind. Sa vie, son œuvre, son époque*, Paris, 1975. — A. HEMINGWAY, *The Norwich School of Painters, 1803-1833*, Oxford, 1979. — K. HERMANN-FIORE, *Dürer Landschaftsaquarelle*, Berne, 1972. — H. HOETINK, *Dürer*, London, 1971. — G. HOLME, *Masters of Water-Colour Painting*, in *The Studio*, special number, London, 1922-1923. — M. HOOG, *L'Univers de Cézanne*, Paris, 1971. — P. HUISMAN, *French Watercolours of the 18th Century*, London and New York, 1969.

P. JAMOT, *Auguste Ravier, étude critique suivie de la correspondance de l'artiste*, Lyons, 1921. — J.C. JENSEN, *Aquarelle und Zeichnungen der deutschen Romantik*, Cologne, 1978.

H. KELLER, *Watercolours and Drawings of the French Impressionists*, New York, 1982. — E. KORNFELD, *Paul Klee in Bern. Aquarelle und Zeichnungen 1897-1915*, Berne, 1973. — W. KOSCHATSKY, *Watercolour: History and Technique*, New York and London, 1970; *Albrecht Dürer: The Landscape Watercolors*, New York, 1973.

L. LAMBOURNE, *British Watercolours in the Victoria and Albert Museum*, London, 1980. — H. LEMAÎTRE, *Le Paysage anglais à l'aquarelle 1760-1851*, Paris, 1955. — J. LEYMARIE, *Gauguin. Watercolours, Pastels and Drawings in Colour*, London, 1961.

K.E. MAISON, *Honoré Daumier. Catalogue Raisonné of the Paintings, Watercolours and Drawings*, 2 vols., London and Greenwich, Conn., 1968. — H.L. MALLALIEU, *The Dictionary of British Water-Colour Artists up to 1920*, London, 1976. — P.L. MATHIEU, *Gustave Moreau, Complete Edition of the Finished Paintings, Watercolours and Drawings*, Oxford and New York, 1977; *Gustave Moreau, Aquarelles*, Fribourg, Switzerland, 1984. — J. MEDER, *Die Handzeichnung, ihre Technik und Entwicklung*, 2nd ed., Vienna, 1923; *The Mastery of Drawing*, 2 vols., New York, 1978. — E. MOREAU-NÉLATON, *Jongkind raconté par lui-même*, Paris, 1918.

C. NISSEN, *Die botanische Buchillustration*, Stuttgart, 1951.

L. PARRIS, *Landscape in Britain 1750-1850*, London, 1973. — D. PATAKY, *Master Drawings from the Collection of the Budapest Museum of Fine Arts, 19th and 20th Centuries*, Budapest and New York, 1959. — L. VAN PUYVELDE, *Van Dyck*, Brussels, 1950.

L. RÉAU, *Un siècle d'aquarelle de Géricault à nos jours*, Paris, 1942. — S. REICH, *John Marin, A Stylistic Analysis and Catalogue Raisonné*, Tucson, Arizona, 1970. — G. REYNOLDS, *A Concise History of Watercolours*, London, 1971. — J. REWALD, *Paul Cézanne, The Watercolors: A Catalogue Raisonné*, New York and London, 1983. — C. ROGER-MARX and S. COTTÉ, *L'Univers de Delacroix*, Paris, 1970.

G. SCHIFF, *Johann Heinrich Füssli*, 2 vols., Zürich, 1973. — J. SELZ, *Dessins et aquarelles du XIXᵉ siècle.*, Naefels, Switzerland, 1976. — M. SERULLAZ, with L. DUCLAUX and G. MONNIER, *Dessins du Louvre, Ecole française*, Paris, 1968. — M. SERULLAZ, *Delacroix*, Paris, 1981. — P. SIGNAC, *Jongkind*, Paris, 1927. — S. SITWELL and W. BLUNT, *Great Flower Books 1700-1900*, London, 1956. — R. STANG, *Edvard Munch, the Man and the Artist*, London, 1979. — D. SUTTON, *French Drawings of the 18th Century*, London, 1949; *Whistler*, London, 1966.

J. TARDIEU, J.C. SCHNEIDER and V. BESSON, *Bazaine*, Paris, 1975.

M. VALSECCHI, *Landscape Painting of the 19th Century*, Greenwich, Conn., 1971.

R. WEDEWER and H. SCHNEIDLER, *Aquarelle und Zeichnungen des 20. Jahrhunderts*, Cologne, 1981. — G. WILDENSTEIN, *Louis Moreau*, Paris, 1923; *Fragonard*, London, 1961. — I.A. WILLIAMS, *Early English Watercolours*, London, 1952. — A. WILSON, *A Dictionary of British Marine Painters*, Leigh-on-Sea, 1967. — A. WILTON, *British Watercolours, 1750 to 1850*, London, 1977; *Life and Work of J.M.W. Turner*, London, 1979.

Principal Exhibitions

1955: *Jongkind, Aquarelles du Dauphiné*, Musée de Peinture et Sculpture, Grenoble. — **1955-1956**: *L'Aquarelle anglaise 1750-1850*, Musée Rath, Geneva. — **1958**: *Disegni inediti della biblioteca comunale di Urbania*, Farnesina, Rome; *20th Century British Watercolours from the Tate Gallery and the Victoria and Albert Museum*, Victoria and Albert Museum, London. — **1958-1959**: *De Clouet à Matisse. Dessins français des collectionneurs américains*, Musée de l'Orangerie, Paris. — **1959**: *Sam Francis, Bilder und Aquarelle 1953-1958*, Galerie Klipstein und Kornfeld, Berne. — **1960**: *Hartung*, Galerie de France, Paris. — **1961**: *Sam Francis, Werke 1960-1961*, Galerie Klipstein und Kornfeld, Berne. — **1962-1963**: *Delacroix*, Art Gallery of Toronto; *Rodin inconnu*, Louvre, Paris. — **1963**: *Eugène Delacroix*, centenary exhibition, Louvre, Paris. — **1964**: *Le dessin français dans les collections hollandaises*, Institut Néerlandais, Paris, and Rijksmuseum, Amsterdam. — **1965**: *Bonington*, Museum and Art Gallery, Nottingham; *August Macke, Handzeichnungen und Aquarelle*, Kunsthalle, Bremen; *Riopelle, Sculpture, Paintings, Watercolors*, Pierre Matisse Gallery, New York. — **1966**: *Peintures et aquarelles anglaises 1700-1900 du Musée de Birmingham*, Musée des Beaux-Arts, Lyons; *Oskar Kokoschka, Aquarelle und Zeichnungen*, Staatsgalerie, Stuttgart; *Mark Tobey, Werke 1933-1966*, Kunsthalle, Berne; *John Marin, Watercolors*, Museum of Modern Art, New York; *Julius Bissier*, Galerie Alice Pauli, Lausanne. — **1966-1967**: *Aquarelles expressionnistes du Wallraf-Richartz Museum de Cologne*, Musée Rath, Geneva. — **1968**: *Romantic Art in Britain. Paintings and Drawings 1760-1860*, Detroit Institute of Arts; *Whistler*, Art Institute of Chicago. — **1968-1969**: *Moderne Zeichnungen und Aquarelle*, Kunstmuseum, Basel. — **1969-1970**: *Sima*, Galerie Engelberts, Geneva. — **1970**: *Julius Bissier*, Galerie Alice Pauli, Lausanne. — **1971**: *Deutsche Zeichnungen und Aquarelle des 19. und 20. Jahrhunderts*, Staatliche Museen, Kupferstichkabinett, East Berlin. — **1972**: *La peinture romantique anglaise et les préraphaélites*, Petit Palais, Paris; *American Watercolors and Drawings from the Museum's Collection*, Rhode Island School of Design, Providence; *Cent dessins du Musée Teyler de Haarlem*, Cabinet des Dessins, Louvre, Paris; *C.D. Friedrich 1774-1840. Romantic Landscape Painting in Dresden*, Tate Gallery, London; *British Watercolors and Drawings from the Museum's Collection*, Rhode Island School of Design, Providence. — **1973**: *Das Aquarell 1400-1950*, Haus der Kunst, Munich; *Old Master Drawings from Chatsworth*, Victoria and Albert Museum, London; *Maurice Estève, aquarelles*, Galerie Claude Bernard, Paris; *English Watercolours of the 18th and 19th Centuries from the Whitworth Art Gallery, Manchester*, Musée d'Art Moderne, Brussels; *Estève, aquarelles*, Neue Galerie Peter Nathan, Zurich. — **1974**: *20th Century Drawings and Watercolours*, Marlborough Gallery, London; *Velins du Museum*, Bibliothèque Albert Ier, Brussels. — **1974-1975**: *Victorian Watercolours from the Collection of the Walker Art Gallery*, Walker Art Gallery, Liverpool. — **1974-1975**: *Turner*, Tate Gallery, London. — **1975**: *French Watercolours and Drawings from the Museum's Collection*, Rhode Island School of Design, Providence; *Die Zeichnungen und Aquarelle des 19. Jahrhunderts in der Graphischen Sammlung*, Staatsgalerie, Stuttgart. — **1976**: *The "Wild Beasts"*, Museum of Modern Art, New York; *Robert Delaunay 1885-1941*, Musée de l'Orangerie, Paris; *André Masson, 200 dessins*, Musée d'Art Moderne de la Ville de Paris; *Constable*, Tate Gallery, London. — **1976-1977**: *Dessins français de l'Art Institute de Chicago, de Watteau à Picasso*, Cabinet des Dessins, Louvre, Paris; *La peinture allemande à l'époque du Romantisme*, Musée de l'Orangerie, Paris; *Women Artists 1550-1950*, Los Angeles County Museum of Art. — **1977**: *Sonia et Robert Delaunay*, Bibliothèque Nationale, Paris; *Collections de Louis XIV. Dessins, albums, manuscrits*, Musée de l'Orangerie, Paris; *Cézanne. The Late Work*, Museum of Modern Art, New York; *Joseph Sima*, Galerie Engelberts, Geneva. — **1978**: *William Blake*, Tate Gallery, London. — **1980**: *Œsterreichische Zeichnungen und Aquarelle des frühen 20. Jahrhunderts aus dem Besitz der Albertina, Wien*, Galerie im Taxispalais, Innsbruck; *Hartung. Œuvres de 1922 à 1939*, Musée d'Art Moderne de la Ville de Paris; *Constantin Guys, il pittore della vita moderna*, Palazzo Braschi, Rome. — **1981**: *Gainsborough*, Grand Palais, Paris; *Turner en France*, Centre Culturel du Marais, Paris; *Jean-Paul Riopelle, 1946-1977*, Centre Georges Pompidou, Paris. — **1981-1982**: *Rodin Rediscovered*, National Gallery of Art, Washington. — **1982**: *Town, Country, Shore and Sea. British Drawings and Watercolours from Anthony Van Dyck to Paul Nash*, Queensland Art Gallery, Brisbane; *Egon Schiele*, Kestner Gesellschaft, Hanover; *Cézanne, Aquarelle*, Kunsthalle, Tübingen, and Kunsthaus, Zürich. — **1983**: *Aquarelle in unserem Jahrhundert*, Kunsthaus, Zug; *L'aquarelle en France au XIXe siècle. Dessins du Musée du Louvre*, Cabinet des Dessins, Louvre, Paris; *Maestri dell'Acquarello Inglese. Acquarelli del Victoria and Albert Museum*, Palazzo Braschi, Rome; *Oskar Kokoschka*, Kestner Gesellschaft, Hanover. — **1983-1984**: *J.M.W. Turner*, Grand Palais, Paris; *Leonardo da Vinci. Natur und Landschaft. Naturstudien aus der Königlichen Bibliothek in Windsor Castle*, Kunsthaus, Zurich; *Honoré Daumier. Georges Rouault*, Académie de France, Rome.

List of illustrations

Index of Names and places